Dreaming a Paradise

THE INDIA LIST

Chitvan Gill

DREAMING
A PARADISE

*Migrations and
the Story of
Buland Masjid*

LONDON NEW YORK CALCUTTA

Seagull Books, 2024

Text and photographs © Chitvan Gill, 2024

ISBN 978 1 80309 380 2

British Library Cataloguing-in-Publication Data
A catalogue record for this book is available from the British Library

Typeset and designed by Seagull Books, Calcutta, India
Printed and bound by Hyam Enterprises, Calcutta, India

Hem & Kanwarpal
Everything
Mama and Daddy
The love will last forever

CONTENTS

ACKNOWLEDGEMENTS

I would like to thank, first and foremost, the kind and generous people of Buland Masjid, whom I met with and who shared their stories with me.

Radhika, thank you for making this book possible, for having faith in me and for all the time you gave, going through the drafts, to help sharpen the manuscript.

Thank you, Naveen, for your encouragement and your generosity in providing me such a distinguished platform for the publication of my first book.

I would also like to thank everyone at Seagull—Sunandini, Diven and Bishan—for their invaluable suggestions and meticulous editing.

My dear friend Teteii, for taking time off from her insanely busy schedules and going through the manuscript twice, for her insightful comments, and for her constant encouragement. My brother Hemant, for all his support, his kindness, for throwing those wonderful dinners for me with Rima and my lovely niece Alina, providing much needed respite and for keeping me in good humour through trying times. Mama, for her love and the joy that she felt at my writing my first book. And special thanks are due to the one who had to suffer, who endured the lunacy, the travails that are a writer's, and held my hand through it all. Thank you, Ajai.

Hartosh, for always believing; thank you for all the help, for devoting much time to the manuscript, and for the gruff, pithy, 'Just keep going'—which did keep me going.

But above all I would like to thank the one who is not here—but always here. Daddy, thank you for the books, for letting us be readers and making me understand at a very early age: a book can save your life.

Build a city and they will come to it.

Who will trace the footsteps of these men, what will they leave in the earth that will tell us they were here?

In a vast landscape of emptiness, carved into the solidified volcanic ash, are the trajectories of life, footprints from 3.6 million years ago. In the dust of centuries that followed, amid the desolation of a desert, a 'rose-red city—half as old as Time'.[1]

In the long, wearing march of infinity, man circles the earth. Always looking to rest in the city he will build.

Here, by the banks of a sacred river, in another rose-red city as old as time, thousands of men left their footprints. Delhi was once the city of seven cities. From antiquity to New Delhi, from gods to emperors, they all came to this rocky red desert, creating new cities to sing of their histories.

In the blinding brightness of our age, millions more continue to march towards this destination. This rushing pulsating megapolis, no longer the blushing rose, no longer the city of seven. All across, every day, a new Delhi is being built. Teetering minarets of ramshackle tenements wobble up towards the sky. The new spawns of civilization,

> [nest] at the end of a tunnel bored by itself in
> a bank.
> [. . .] on fishbones
> not on bare clay, on bones thrown up in pellets by
> the birds.
> On these rejectamenta
> [. . .] the young are born.
> And, as they are fed and grow, this nest of
> excrement and decayed fish becomes
> a dripping, fetid mass.[2]

Each dripping fetid mass is a new city, an Eden built by those who have endured migrations through hell. They redefine and reshape paradise on earth to a modern incarnation. In one such Eden, Buland Masjid, we hear the story of the men who walked all the way to this bleak and hostile piece of land, to create a place they could eventually call home.

Men, who had tried to stay, rooted in the hearth of ancient love and blood. But the earth had turned against them, leaving the dry scab of indifference all around. These Odysseys of flight, from hunger, from fear, that search for life, for new beginnings, hold within them the story of mankind. The wanderings of man echo a ritual as old as time. From a hidden corner of Delhi to the vastness of the world; the dust of the earth swirls with the million migrations that have written that ageless story.

THE MIGRATION

In *The Descent of Man* (1871), Darwin writes:

> But the most curious instance known to me of one instinct getting the better of another is the migratory instinct conquering the maternal instinct. The former is wonderfully strong; a confined bird will at the proper season beat her breast against the wires of her cage, until it is bare and bloody. It causes young salmon to leap out of the fresh water, in which they could continue to exist, and thus unintentionally to commit suicide. Everyone knows how strong the maternal instinct is, leading even timid birds to face great danger, though with hesitation, and in opposition to the instinct of self-preservation. Nevertheless, the migratory instinct is so powerful, that late in the autumn swallows, house-martins, and swifts frequently desert their tender young, leaving them to perish miserably in their nests.[3]

The human imagination is obsessed with the idea of leaving: 'If I stay here any longer, I will die.' The idea, the impetus to survival, is rooted within this. To go someplace else is the ambition of the Id. Yet the surging contradictions that are held within this idea wrench the deepest core of existence. From the very beginnings of life, the idea of leaving and arriving has consumed the making of the human, from the single cell to man as we know him. A curious, perverse and primal tic dictates the nature of life, and within this continuum lies its eternal tragedy.

From the oldest migrations, where all love was left behind as Adam and Eve were expelled from Eden, their naked bodies adorned with shame. Banished from the idyllic world they embark upon a search for a new beginning. To recreate paradise, you must journey through hell. William Blake's illustrations of *Paradise Lost*,[4] of their expulsion, capture the catastrophic horror of the moment, the shame and fear, the tense cringing of the muscles, as the biblical couple leaves, cursed to a life of strife and doom.

> And the Lord said to Cain, 'Where is Abel your brother?' And he said, 'I do not know: am I my brother's keeper?' And He said, 'What have you done? Listen! your brother's blood cries out to me from the soil. And so, cursed shall you be by the

soil that gaped with its mouth to take your
brother's blood from your hand. If you till the soil,
it will no longer give you strength. A restless
wanderer shall you be on the earth.'[5]

Original sin compounded by the first murder. Man lives,
caught in the chakra of his actions, tormented with the
pain of wandering, hanging on to a sliver of hope, of
belief. And paradise is always a city, the creation of man
in all its splendour. Cain, the slayer of his brother—the
first murderer, the cursed wanderer—builds the city of
Enoch.

Expulsion and reinvention . . . these themes suffuse
the human narrative, right from the earliest epics. All the
stories of faith, the myths and legends that sustain
mankind, find a universal resonance in the narration of
this cycle of doom and redemption. The tale of man is the
long walk, escaping hunger, conflict, strife, seeking happiness, a new beginning.

Gilgamesh the tall, magnificent and terrible,
    who opened passes in the mountains,
who dug wells on the slopes of the uplands,
    and crossed the ocean, the wide sea to the
    sunrise;
who scoured the world ever searching for life,

and reached through sheer force Uta-napishti
the Distant;
who restored the cult-centres destroyed by the
Deluge,
and set in place for the people the rites of the
cosmos.[6]

From the oldest of written epics, the Epic of Gilgamesh, narrating the stirring tales of the great king and his wanderings that take him to the very edge of the world and back, carved onto great tablets of terracotta, buried under millennia of dust, unearthed centuries later, to the Biblical retelling of man and his fate.

Themes spoken of centuries ago find resonance in the modern world. Sebastião Salgado's epic journeys bear witness to the unbearable paradoxes of beauty and unyielding cruelty that mark this indifferent universe. The photographs of the great famine and futile migrations of the Ethiopians in search of food, of life, echo the wanderings of mankind, endured through all of time.

From the hallucinatory heroic wanderings of Don Quixote, where Cervantes takes us through a journey of the mind, to a young Naipaul's arrival in London, a man marked by the journeys of his ancestors, whose own restless passion for questing created his own legacy. The histories of worlds left behind, of places where it is impossible to be heard any longer. Men, cast out, driven away, escaping certain death, write through memories. They write of loss and loneliness, of landscapes of love, of forests, hills, mountains, rivers that flowed through their soul. Driven out by hate, by tyranny, writers, artists, struggle to remember, to forget, fragmented memories, as they are forced to endure expulsions from lands that sustained and nurtured their imaginations.

In an ancient age, under the dark mantle of the night sky, a young man crept out of his home, leaving a young woman and an infant sleeping in their beds. The young prince, or Siddharth as he was called, spent the rest of his life trying to uncover the answers to illuminate the futile life of man. He journeyed, walking, questing, till the moment of truth, the enlightenment. His journey from Siddhartha to the Buddha led him to the idea of the salvation of man . . . 'No one saves us, but ourselves. No one can and no one may: We ourselves must walk the path.'[7]

Such men have always walked the earth, men driven by that same impetus, to ease the sufferings of mankind. Moses, Jesus, Mohammed, Adi Shankara or Nanak, they have walked from one edge of their lands to another, seeking new answers to age-old questions, renewing ancient faiths.

When Lucy set out on her long walk, did this our ancestor leave a paradise or go out in search of one? She lay in the vast loneliness, waiting for the men who scour the earth and rake through the dust of time, the striate of lines carved into unyielding rock, the ocean beds, the bones of man, to uncover the long journeys of the past, to make sense of the present. Food, they said, food was what Lucy had embarked in search of. Lucy's migrations left the story of man imprinted in her bones, that astonishing story, the feat of this being, the calculations of cells, circuits and the slippery slime that lay encased in the hardness of its skull, that pushed it through an aeon of agonizing contortions to follow the simple instruction: 'Get up, stand up and walk'. Centuries later, that little frame of the young girl, with the white eggs of crocodiles and turtles near her, tells us how we as a species dominate the story of this earth today. Those men also tell us that elephants walk back hundreds of miles to caress the bones of their dead, sifting through the dusty earth and showering themselves with the shards in the white ash. These are their sacred places, their pilgrimages ending in these gentle, quiet rituals to celebrate the memories of their loved ones.

Every winter, eight black-necked cranes migrate from Tibet to the flood plains of the Nyamjang Chu River in the Tawang district of India's Arunachal Pradesh. Their survival hinges on this yearly migration. This is their paradise, their place of creation. If they end this migration or are forced out of this paradise, the wide span of their white wings will no longer rustle through the azure skies, casting shadows on the sacred mountains.

The world drifts across oceans. Man walks from continent to continent. Animals, birds, trees, plants, all the stuff of life that bursts forth, is carried into virgin lands awaiting the arrival of this animal, waiting to feed his hunger.

In *The Ascent of Man* (1973), Jacob Bronowski describes the yearly migration of the Bakhtiari:

> What happens to the old when they cannot cross
> the last river? Nothing. They stay behind to die.
> Only the dog is puzzled to see a man abandoned.
> The man accepts the nomad custom; he has come
> to the end of his journey, and there is no place at
> the end.[8]

Women, widows, young and old, who are left behind, cast out, pick a lonely trail in one of the most inhuman migrations known to man. These wisps of white shuffle

towards their eventual destination—the holy city of
Vrindavan, wretched with the moral filth of its devotees
who have turned that embodiment of faith and sanctuary
into one of the most hideous manifestations of indifference,
cruelty and exploitation. Hundreds of women straggle in
and fling their wretched, tired, skeletons into any corner of
refuge they can find. They live out their lives here, bearing
the cross of a fight they never sought, paying the price for
the death of a man they knew in the way they were told:
'God willed it.'

Every night in this wretched sad land there are a billion
dreams. The night tosses people, half awake, half asleep,
stretched guts gnawing with hunger, tired, racked bodies
wailing for respite . . . to sleep, to dream. As the dog howls
into the lonely night, a few men steel their resolve, some
rouse themselves to quietly steal into the night, walking
and then running till their shadows finally leave. The
morning sees men suddenly propelled by the wet
tenderness held tight in the lungs, run slow hands across
the withered cheeks of mothers and casting a last glance
to the young woman and a wailing child held aloft. This
is what is—who knows what can be?

At the end, we can only speak of our wanderings, of
our search, of the exodus, or the solitary quest.

Mothers who don't know where their sons have gone or if they will ever see them again. The son sits, a faded photograph, his mother's face beautiful from a long time ago, lies crushed as he carries it from one place to another.

A man can watch an apple fall, a bolt of lightning streak across the sky, and unlock the secrets of the void. The leaps and bounds, the circularity of the imagination, allows man to survive and to go further and further into the frontiers of the unknown. The darkness of the self seeks comfort beyond the abyss. The gold of the constellation lures him—there, perhaps, is the paradise lost? In an effort to reach his destination and subdue the salty ache of existence he can resort to unheard-of cruelties, forcing others to go before him to discover longed-for truths.

The starlings fill the skies, thousands in flight, enacting the poetic dance of life. Back and forth, upwards and down, swooping, swirling, they follow each other in an unrehearsed yet minutely orchestrated waltz. Their murmuration, an etching of the life of man, a frenetic moment in time, and then, just as suddenly, all is ceased. The sky is clear—the birds are gone.

Three days before the scheduled liftoff, Laika entered her constricted travel space that allowed for only a few inches of movement. Newly cleaned, armed with sensors, and fitted with a sanitation device, she wore a spacesuit with metal restraints built-in. On November 3 at 5:30 a.m., the ship lifted off with G-forces reaching five times normal gravity levels. The noises and pressures of flight terrified Laika: Her heartbeat rocketed to triple the normal rate, and her breath rate quadrupled. [. . .] Unfortunately, loss of the heat shield made the temperature in the capsule rise unexpectedly, taking its toll on Laika. She died 'soon after launch', Russian medical doctor and space dog trainer Oleg Gazenko revealed in 1993. 'The temperature inside the spacecraft after the fourth orbit registered over 90 degrees', [Cathleen] Lewis says. [. . .] Without its passenger, Sputnik 2 continued to orbit for five months.[9]

2

MAQSOOD: CREATING A DESTINY

Where a man runs, hope waking in his breast,
For ever like a madman, seeking rest.[10]

He must have died happy, for all around him was his creation, his paradise. Rising out of the swampy marsh now buried under solid concrete, was his city, the city he had built. The streets clearly demarcated, grid patterns or katras, the imposition of order, of discipline. He died in his paradise.

Maqsood, a man who spat in the face of destiny, walked from the abyss to arrive at this place, where he began his own story of creation.

He had walked quickly and then run across the dusty plains, chased by hunger, battling the raging heat of the sun and the fire of a slow, burning anger within.

Hunger gnaws the bones, it corrodes the thin epithelial linings of the innards, but hunger propels the world into existence.

Maqsood walked into Delhi with nothing. And within his lifetime, he created this . . .

I came to his paradise. What was this that he had created? What could one say about it? He sat on his charpai—inhaling the rancid tar of his beedi, dragging deep, his eyes half shut—and exhaled in two gusts. The smoke from his lungs and the blistering beedi created delicate wisps and swirls and gently wafted upwards to join the thick smog, the stinking fog, the acrid haze of burning waste that rose from the landfill. He raised his arm and moved it in a sweeping arc: 'All this I have done, this is the labour of my life.' This was the culmination of one man's passion, his search for a home, for a paradise of rest, of love and hope.

All around was shit, rotting entrails, refuse and the leavings of the stuff of the urban dream. Here in these tee-tering tenements is a story as old as man. 'How terrible it would have been [. . .] to have lived without even attempting to lay claim to one's portion of the earth; to have lived and died as one had been born, unnecessary and unaccommodated.'[11]

Maqsood left behind a house and a legacy. This man, who walked here with nothing, transformed his world. Eschewing the symbols of wealth, the ornaments of 'arrival' that proclaimed success to the world, he looked inward. It was the spirit of yearning, of trying to understand how to tame the beast of nature, the crudeness of raw reality, to transform the power of desire into a spirit of beauty.

I met him one day as I walked through the gallis of this slum called Buland Masjid. He was seated, as was his wont, on a charpai outside his tenement. Around him was clustered a group of men, listening to him in respectful silence. As I walked past, he softly hailed me: 'I'm sorry I cannot get up, I have a bad leg, but I have seen you coming here for the past few days, I am very intrigued, and if you don't mind telling me: what are you doing in this place?' I told him. Immediately the men around him turned to me and said, 'But you must talk to him, he is the one you must talk to. He is Allama Maqsood, he is the one who built this colony.' Maqsood looked at me and said softly, 'Yes, they are right. If that is the case, then you must talk to me.' This was said without the slightest touch of arrogance or humility, just matter of fact, with a tinge of surprise as to how I had not done so till now.

He exuded a raw physicality, marked with the frailty of age. The eyes, which, at some point of time, would have been hard with steely determination, were softened now with the essence of a man who had faced his demons.

I often sat there, listening to him, eliciting the tales of his life. Maqsood told his story with a certain wryness; in his mind, he carried the knowledge of what it had taken to arrive at his dream.

'Oh yes, I have not forgotten. I remember violence. I remember when it struck my cheek for the first time, it was not just the physical pain but the mind which ran on to create the pain. That is what I remember . . . I had no control over that. I learnt quickly that there were different types of violence that ordinary people could inflict. Kicking, pummelling, being tossed about on the dry and dusty ground, a bunch of snivelling gigglers gathered around . . . But that was not as hurtful. Strangely, my mind's eye would be casting around, gazing at their faces, and I would forget my pain when I would see in the eyes of some of the young boys neither revelry nor support, but a sense of suspended emotion, a sort of held-in-the-breath, unspoken hope . . . That one boy battled more than five and kept getting up. It was as if they were waiting for some other narrative to emerge from the ritual.

'But what I remember is the violence of words, of flung insults that called to mind a painful inescapable reality, a reality that had been imposed upon me . . . The sheer pain of the relatively painless act of being spat upon, and feeling the slow crawl of saliva dripping down my bloodied cheeks. Nothing hurt more than that. My life is almost over, but the act of being spat upon, from the moment when you see his face prepare, to the gentle settling of spit on the cheek . . . I can never forget the sheer pain of that moment or the face of that man.

'The word I remember most is *Muslim*. Within the sound of that word is wrapped the story of my life, the violence, and sense of raging impotence, whenever I heard that word flung at me. As if I was not a human—I was a Muslim. "Tum Mussalman ho".'

But violence was everywhere. There was no escaping. It was a violence of the soul. A battle between hunger and hope. The sheer violence that visited the failure of mothers, of fathers as they struggled to hide their inability to give their children the lives they had hoped for . . .

'Hope. I learnt early on, to crawl out of an abyss—it would have to be done without the sentimental crutch of hope.

'My parents were good people, simple, uneducated. My father tutored in the basics of survival and the rudimentary aspects of raising a family. And that he tried to do. He was told he had to be a provider, he was a good man. But he was unable to battle hunger and poverty, and

15

his impotence as he saw my bruised battered face, body, slowly ate away at his reservoirs of strength, of fight. What he did have, what everyone like him had, in the village, and the next, and miles around till it became an immeasurable whole, was faith. Increasingly everyone would become seemingly bent—the spirit sucked out of their youthful frames—and hold their hands out in a plea, a supplication to a void, appealing with fervour for deliverance.

'And I am thankful they had that. From within that void they heard the voice of creation and continuance and somehow derived the strength to keep going, to survive.

'In my village, there was nothing to eat, to drink, the earth squeezed dry of water, of sustenance. What we did see as children was the young men leaving, some never to return. A few returned but only for a briefness, bearing gifts of momentary diversion, which the children kept as cherished objects in memory of the men they rarely saw . . . A few came back looking stronger, determined, and gathered the ragtag collection of humans that made up their family and left. Forever. We never saw them again.

'I knew then that I must leave. I do not know at what moment such a thought strikes you, whether it lingers like an irksome itch, or it suddenly dawns upon you. Now it seems inexplicable how an eight-year-old boy was able to work out that he would have to leave the embrace of his mother to find a life—to stay alive.

'Early one morning I woke up while everyone was still asleep and slowly, softly, I crept out. I took nothing with me, except the clothes on my back.'

At this point Maqsood stopped. He fell silent, looked away as if he had suddenly withdrawn into a world of his own, one to which we were denied access. A silence descends in the room. His room, with its green walls, a yellow-and-black photograph of the Kaaba hanging above his bed. The built-in shelves, a few plastic flowers in a plastic vase, steel utensils, a collection of books and, most precious of all, his folders, the accumulation of his life's work, sheaves of documents essaying his struggle to build and legalize the Buland Masjid colony. Prayer beads hang from another shelf. It is the austere room of a man of faith.

It is the hour of the azan, he turns to me and tells me to stop recording. 'You will not be able to hear anything.'

At eventide, the muezzin's voice rings out through the loudspeakers atop the mosque, calling the believers to prayer. Maqsood's house is a few metres away from the masjid and the call is deafening. The lilting melody holds you, yet you are close to a sense of relief when it ends. I turn towards him, expecting him to start again. He holds up his hand, 'Wait,' he says, and then it comes again, from a different direction. Five minutes later, yet again. Each call through its own set of loudspeakers, resounding across the colony and beyond.

What is happening?

Majid, a young boy who has just joined us, starts giggling. 'They're all rival factions, each with their own mosque. They stagger their timings to establish their own identity.'

Maqsood is impassive. 'Dhongi hain sare,' is his quiet comment. They are all posers. It is an introduction to the corruption of faith once it falls into the hands of the untrue. It is also an insight into Maqsood's vision of faith and belief. He sought his own accommodation with the One, refusing the intermediaries of faith, the power of intervention and interference. The contemplation of the divine helped him survive those journeys, it was quiet, it was profound. Perhaps it was this accommodation that allowed him to become the man he was.

It was startling to encounter such spirit, such fearlessness, such quiet strength. There was a disdain that coloured his outlook whenever he spoke of the men who were supposed to be the harbingers of comfort, whether it be in faith or the men of the secular world with their promises of material deliverance from suffering.

'No one from these parties has ever done anything for us. We did everything by ourselves. No one, neither the old party nor the new one that claims to be for the people. In fact, they never come here. All these people just show their faces when they need our votes.

'People have fragile reservoirs of endurance, they are willing to believe anything, anyone. In fact, it is the people who are at fault—they give up the struggle and abandon themselves to false prophets, to men.'

'Shiksha,' he says, 'I realized that it was only the world of knowledge that would lead people out of this. I learnt this very early on in life. What I witnessed and endured in my father's home, in the village, made me understand this truth.'

In my days and time spent in Buland Masjid, I hear his name again and again. 'Allama-ne bahut sacrifice kiye hain is colony ke liye'—Allama has sacrificed a lot for this colony.

I have to keep returning to him for his story, and for the story of Buland Masjid.

'Yes. I am proud of what I have done. Why should we be forced to live like criminals? It is not a crime to be born poor. What they do to the poor is the crime. I fought, I went to court, I filed cases, I asked for water, electricity, sewage drains, ration cards. I got people onto voters' lists, I got the layout plan drafted and submitted. It was not easy, it was a huge struggle, but I persisted, I refused to give in.'

By now a relationship of mutual warmth has developed between us. 'I like it when you visit us here,' he says, 'when you visit our colony.' On my part I take away so much from this man, his struggles and his story . . .

His home was always abuzz with activity. I would often find him in his room with four, five men from the colony, files and papers spread around him on his charpai. He showed me documents, appeals and applications to the Delhi Development Authority, the DDA. 'This is the evidence of my struggle.' Often, he would be dictating and one of the men would be taking notes. On one such occasion, he introduced me to a couple of them. 'This is Kamran, the treasurer, and this is a local schoolteacher, Iqbal. These are the men who have helped in the struggle, they prepare all my drafts and appeals for me according to what I tell them. No one had any idea how to go about getting a case prepared and presented. And I was handicapped by my inability to read and write.'

The man who was only addressed as Allama, a title given to a person of great scholarship and erudition, was completely illiterate.

'Yes,' he says, looking at my stunned expression, 'I was never allowed to complete my studies, I had to drop out in the third standard. Forced to leave, driven out of school. "You cannot study. Tum Mussalman ho. Mussalman ko padh ke kya karna?"' You're a Muslim. What's a Muslim going to get out of studying?

It was this painful denial, this violent eviction of a young child from what was rightfully his—an education—that left a deep scar in his psyche. The young Maqsood carried the burden, the absence of the possibility of hope, of escape.

But he fought his severe poverty and educated all his children. Today his young son works in a software company. His daughter and daughter-in-law are teachers. His home is filled with the team of members he has gathered under the NGO which he founded and which helps run the colony.

'This place is filled with the despair and the suffering of poverty. Drugs, criminality, prostitution . . . you name it, you will find it here. I realized that people need a more concrete way to seek help rather than false, empty promises. That is why I started this NGO.'

But that is now. Young Maqsood stopped running when he reached this city of plenty. 'I felt neither fear nor awe. Yes, the scale, the noise, was overwhelming, but it was the wealth, the sheer wealth—that a place like this could exist and people could live in such indifference to the suffering of others!'

He speaks of those years as an inevitable rite of passage. 'It was hard, but I had a fire, a hunger within, which kept burning. I worked, I laboured, I taught myself in the evenings. You will find many stories such as mine all over this city. We make our own fate. Some never live to tell their tale, I survived. I found a home.

'Beneath these floors is the dry sand of the Yamuna River. This is where I eventually came as a young man. Here I found thousands of men cast out of their homes by poverty, by distress migration. It was on these banks of the Yamuna that we found a place to put up a shelter. This is where I lay down for years, my place of rest.

'There was nothing other than the swampy mud to lie upon and a plastic sheet to cover us. Here I saw and heard the despair and madness of men who now had food in their belly yet who howled into the blackness of the night, driven insane by demons, by loneliness. I don't know what would have happened to me if she had not come into my life.'

Armed with nothing but determination, he found strength in what he could never thank Allah enough for. His wife.

He shows me a photograph taken shortly after their marriage. Two individuals in the prime of their youth, shy and beautiful, so beautiful, faces that bear nothing but the will to be guided by goodness. 'This is she,' he says with pride as he turns towards his wife sitting quietly in a corner of the room. 'If she had not come into my life,' he pauses, overcome with emotion, 'it would all have been different. I would not be the man they tell you I am. It is only with her help that I was able to keep going with the struggle. The struggle for Buland Masjid, to make this home our little paradise. None of it would have been possible without her. When we came, there was nothing. Only empty marshland owned by poor farmers. I acquired some land from them with the money I earned with my labours in this city. It was dirt cheap. No one was willing to come, let alone live, here. But these were the banks of our Yamuna. Together, the two of us spent hours labouring to turn the marshy land into a foundation upon which we could build a jhuggi. But whatever we did it would be ours. It would belong to us.'

Maqsood introduces me to his son, Suleiman. His impassive face struggles to control the pride he takes in his son's achievement. Suleiman works with a multi-national IT company, and also helps his father with his NGO. He's a clean-cut young man, extremely pleasant, with a lovely wife and three beautiful young children. They are well-settled, the quintessential happy family.

Then, on one of my later visits, it is Suleiman who tells me, 'Abba ka inteqal ho gaya.' Father has passed away.

I retreated homewards. I did not know what to say to the young man.

———•———

I stood looking at Maqsood's world. That men should have to live in such squalor. There was no escaping the visible filth, the complete degradation of this urban settlement. It was the stink of indifference that was everywhere. That there were men not far from here who had the power to change it all, men who had been entrusted with the sworn duty to deliver a mandate of justice, of equality. Those very men allowed these purgatories to flourish. A defeated temper allowed these men to cultivate a culture of criminal apathy.

In the bitter chill, winter fires glowed, as men, women and children clustered around. The heat shimmer cast their bodies into a wavering ephemerality. Perhaps this could be the glimmering of a new revolution.

For Maqsood, this was a world from which he had eventually derived joy and purpose, that rose above the ordinary. He had moved from the primeval need for survival to the spiritual, a world in which he made peace with hope and left his legacy with his children, cleansed of the horrors of survival, of the darkness that lurks within the human spirit. They would not have to grasp for happiness—he had handed it to them.

3

BULAND MASJID

A journey is a fragment of hell.

[T]he migration itself, like the pilgrimage, is the
hard journey: a 'leveler' on which the 'fit' survive
and stragglers fall by the wayside.[12]

Then they all gathered one evening. They said: we have
nothing, but we have our place of divinity, and we are
thankful for that. This, what we have, what we are
making. We shall dedicate it to the divine, and we shall
call it Buland Masjid.

Buland Masjid is the story of migrations into hell, and
they end in a struggle to create a paradise.

Perhaps this, here, is paradise.

This magnificent city of eight and half acres, full of the
raw effluvia of man. Piss, shit, food, shame, fear, hunger,
pride, exertion, the searing heat of hatred, anger, and the
brief calming temper of love and sustenance. Behind every
decrepit shanty, every soaring tenement, is an epic journey,
the spirit of men who have struggled and survived.

I came upon this city by chance.

Humanity abounds here. Men, women and children scurry out of every nook and alley, the narrow passages barely able to contain the ongoing rush of human traffic. These are the ants in their anthills, fragile yet secure in a place of their own. There is the same driving rush of energy, of industry. What was a listless heap of bone, flesh and blood, is now transformed into an embodiment of a leap of faith.

What is this city here, in this little bowl of land hidden behind tall white buildings? This was land where the sacred river Yamuna once flowed. She has been moved away, forced to abandon the dark muddy slime of her womb, as a refuge for the destitute, the homeless. She now flows, in her new, constrained space, further down. She, the mighty Yamuna, daughter of the great sun god, loved and revered, venerated from the beginning of time. Once joyous, beautiful, unfettered, now yoked in, wearing signs of severe abuse and neglect. Today, the sacred river is a quiet, slow-moving sludge of raw shit and toxic froth, a large sewer cutting through this city of antiquity. On the other side lies the sacred, legendary city of the god-kings, the warrior Pandavas. Here, on the east side or Jamnapaar, is Maqsood's city. One of the thousands of rumble-tumble accretions that, cobbled together, comprise what is called East Delhi.

To enter this world is to enter a theatre playing out the sublime tragedy of man. The quiet stolidity of the butcher, his shirt drenched in blood, his face marked by the darkness and light of human existence. The gentle calmness of his stare at odds with the deep scar running down his face, his nose hacked off from one side, some-where, sometime in his journeys before . . . he sits there, serene and impervious, with his beautiful young wife beside him, a wooden cart before them, heaped with poul-try carcasses. They have done their time; their wanderings are now over.

Elsewhere, amid pigs and goats and animal entrails, she sits, a young girl, in the first flush of her youthful beauty. Slim, tall, endowed with a natural elegance, her head covered with a wispy white veil embroidered with flowers, her face bent low, she concentrates, her delicate fingers moving a thin needle and skein of thread over a trim of delicate lace . . . She is of those who opened their eyes in Buland Masjid and have known no other world. Her parents named her Razida.

The children of Buland Masjid are the children of a new world. They are settlers' children. You can tell them apart from those who are not born to Buland Masjid. There is a confidence that sets them apart. The cheeks are filled out, with the slight oily patina of health that oozes from the pores of their skin. Young boys and girls walk tall, assertive. They are already being pulled into the numbing stupefaction, the pleasing wellness of bourgeois life . . . Within the space of a generation, they have been separated from the memories, the wretchedness and travails that marked the lives of their parents

Young boys come and go, their motorcycles revving though the alleys, bursting pods of energy, enjoying the fruits of the labours of their fathers, and their fathers before.

A young boy grins shyly. I engage in a conversation with him. His father, Shamim, is busy slashing and cutting, engaged in the chores of a butcher's work. Saqib wears an apron and stands away from the shop. He is reluctant to take part in the business, his features delicate and his hair styled in a manner that I almost mistake him for a young girl. I ask if he would like to be photographed and talk to me at length. He tells me to meet him the next day. We agree to meet in the newly opened Changezi Dhaba. I wait for him. He is late. Several phone calls and almost three quarters of an hour later, he arrives on a swank white motorcycle with another young boy riding pillion. He apologizes: 'We got delayed at the salon. This is Sam.'

'Yes, but,' I ask, 'what is his real name?'

They break into giggles, 'Salman.'

I ask Shamim's son if he would like to continue his father's trade. 'Not at all, I am going to be a film star. I am going to Bombay to join films. There is nothing else I want to do. Films are my passion. I want to emulate my hero, my inspiration—Salman Khan.'

In an alley, an old bearded man, Afsar Qureshi, his features bearing the ancestral contours of men from the high passes, still carrying a blunted handsomeness, his sloe eyes the colour of dull, grey, moisture-laden skies, sits in a tiny hovel and carves out chunks of meat on a curved knife held between his toes. He is preparing for the evening, when his little cubbyhole will suddenly be transformed into one of the most in-demand kebab stalls. This morning, however, he surveys me balefully, 'Things are not going well for me, these are bad days.'

The evening brings swarms of little children and young men to his makeshift dhaba. His young daughter steps out. She is dressed in a black tight-fitting salwar kameez, her head covered with a black dupatta. She is strikingly attractive, the beauty of the mohalla. She positions herself behind her father, and engages in flirtatious banter with the admiring young men. I ask if I may take her photograph. She refuses. I move away, and photograph her father and the people who come and go. She quietly moves in front of my camera. I worry about her request and move towards a welding unit on the other side of the galli. She hops across and engages the workers in familiar chit-chat. I now deliberately take a photograph of her, 'Aap ka photo le-liya hai main-ne.' I have taken a photograph of you. She giggles. She suddenly has no objections. It was the fear of being photographed in front of her father that had made her refuse. She is now happily posing and smiling for me. There is a sense of bitter sweetness—her eagerness to be photographed, yet be a 'good' girl. Her natural exuberance, her pleasure in her beauty, her sense of that little glimpse of power that comes with that beauty. If she could, she would let her beauty speak for her. But she knows that is not possible. This world of stragglers, of admiring young men, is where it will bloom and slowly fade, and with it, the fires of unrealized dreams.

All around are images of poverty, aspiration and efforts to transcend. The new generation dares to dream longer and harder than their parents. They will leave this ghetto, they will escape this hell.

They take me to a little hall. Several boys and young men from the colony are lined up to greet me. They stand there, birds of paradise, their hair styled into vivid displays of imaginative fervour, gleaming, shimmering colours, tints of gold, red, yellow, blue, teased into stiff upright puffs or loose waves, golden orange locks falling down their foreheads, getting into their eyes. Some have shorn-off eyebrows, some pencil-shaped arches tweaked, primped, trussed, plucked, their cheeks buffed to a glistening sheen . . . earrings, studs, necklaces, chains, bracelets. Their clothes are a testament to originality and a tribute to their hero, Salman Khan. Metallic jackets, tight jeans, ripped, adorned with the faces of popular rap artists, heeled boots, each boy is a self-created artist, each a vivid painting willing you to view it seriously. Somebody puts on some music that makes the walls reverberate, suddenly everyone begins spinning, twisting, jumping and rolling about the floor. Whatever this exhibition is, you cannot help being swept away by the sheer force of all this energy, these overflowing reservoirs of adrenaline.

Here in this cramped space, watching this enthusiastic dancing, I am reminded of a description of another slum and another young boy nearly two centuries ago.

On his visit to New York, Charles Dickens visited the slum colony, Five Points. In *American Notes* (1842), he gives his account of his trip. Here he describes the exuberant talent of the Black star dancer, Master Juba.

> Single shuffle, double shuffle, cut and cross-cut; snapping his fingers, rolling his eyes, turning in his knees, presenting the backs of his legs in front, spinning about on his toes and heels like nothing but the man's fingers on the tambourine; dancing with two left legs, two right legs, two wooden legs, two wire legs, two spring legs—all sorts of legs and no legs—what is this to him?[13]

Master Juba came to be known as the 'inventor of tap dancing'.[14] Will any Master Jubas emerge from Buland Masjid?

What was Five Points?

> About 200 years ago, Lower Manhattan was adorned by a pretty five-acre lake known as the Collect [. . .] By the mid-1700s, however, the Collect was already rimmed with slaughterhouses and tanneries. The effusions from these bloody businesses were poured directly into the lake and more industries, more trash, quickly followed. By 1800, the Collect was a reeking cesspool [. . .] and by 1825 something entirely new stood on the site—America's first real slum, the Five Points.[15]

'[A]ll that is loathsome, drooping and decayed is here,' an appalled Dickens wrote.[16]

Today, Five Points includes the areas known as Little Italy, Chinatown and what contains the courthouses of Manhattan. This iconic space of urban history saw and gave shelter to the unending waves of immigrants that crowded into the city, the freed slaves, the Irish, Italian, Chinese, all found shelter in this slum. It was where the dispossessed and the poor built their lives of escape.

If the slums of New York fascinated Dickens, then his own city of London occupied much of his concerns.

On 5 July 1849, the *Times* published a letter under the headline 'A Sanitary Remonstrance', signed by 54 people, inhabitants of a cellar in St Giles.

THE EDITUR OF THE TIMES PAPER

Sur,—May we beg and beseech your proteckshion and power. We are Sur, as it may be, livin in a Wilderniss, so far as the rest of London knows anything of us, or as the rich and great people care about. We live in muck and filth. We aint got no priviz, no dust bins, no drains, no water-splies, and no drain or suer in the hole place. The Suer Company, in Greek St., Soho Square, all great, rich and powerfool men, take no notice watsomdever of our complaints. The Stenche of a Gully-hole is disgustin. We all of us suffer, and numbers are ill, and if the Colera comes Lord help us.

Some gentlemans comed yesterday, and we thought they was comishioners from the Suer Company, but they was complaining of the noosance and stenche our lanes and corts was to them in New Oxforde Strect. They was much surprized to see the seller in No. 12, Carrier St., in our lane, where a child was dyin from fever, and would not believe that Sixty persons sleep in it every night. This here seller you couldent swing a cat in, and the rent is five shillings a week; but theare are greate many sich deare sellars. Sur, we hope you will let us have our complaints put into your hinfluenshall paper, and make these landlords of our houses and these comishioners (the friends we spose of the landlords) make our houses decent for Christions to live in. Preaye Sir com and see us, for we are living like piggs, and it aint faire we shoulde be so ill treted.

We are your respeckfull servents in Church Lane, Carrier St., and the other corts. Teusday, Juley 3, 1849.[17]

The poignant nakedness of the articulation lends a certain power to the appeals of these hapless residents.

The conditions of the slums of London forced Dickens to engage with their inhuman realities in several of his novels and writings. George Bernard Shaw saw fit to plunge into the world of municipal governance—he was a municipal councillor on the St Pancras vestry, and served on public health, parliamentary, electricity, housing and drainage committees. In a letter, he writes,

Instead of belonging to a literary club I belong to a municipal council. Instead of drinking and discussing authors and reviews I sit on committees with capable practical greengrocers and bookmakers and administer the collection of dust, the electric lighting of the streets and the enforcement of the sanitary laws.[18]

The slums were the spinoffs of the industrial revolution, and the city was gorged with this scourge. Marx and Engels, on their visit to London slums, were horrified by the condition of these rabbit warrens.

In *The Condition of the Working Class in London* (1845), Engels writes:

This colossal centralisation [. . .] has raised London to the commercial capital of the world [. . .] all this is so vast, so impressive, that a man cannot collect himself, but is lost in the marvel of England's greatness before he sets foot upon English soil.

[. . .] [But] after visiting the slums of the metropolis, one realises for the first time that these Londoners have been forced to sacrifice the best qualities of their human nature, to bring to pass

all the marvels of civilisation which crowd their
city. [. . .] The brutal indifference, the unfeeling
isolation of each in his private interest, becomes
the more repellent and offensive, the more these
individuals are crowded together, within a limited
space.[19]

That was written in 1845. Here in this corner of Delhi,
hundreds of years later, we find almost the same circumstances prevailing.

———•———

Young Razida's father, Pir Baksh, sired seven children. Pir
Baksh stands out in the rumble-jumble of the crowd. There
is something about his mien, gentle and kind; a quixotic
air of benevolence marks his features. His little shop, which
also doubles as extra living quarters, is unlike the others.
Sacks and piles of coal, goats, beds, a makeshift kitchen,
shelves stocked with food and utensils, a small chair and
table, all jostle for space. Next to a bed is an iron safe with
the auspicious number 786 painted across it. He sits in
front of the shack, cross-legged, a neat arrangement of eggs
in trays piled atop each other; there is a little stove in front

of him, a saucepan bubbles, eggs are boiled and served to waiting customers. His enterprises are unlike any of the others. His own unique business ventures. I could see him as an adventurer on an epic journey. What inspires and drives the lives of men? Hunger? Survival? His family of eight bustled in and out as he narrated his journey from Khurja in Uttar Pradesh, to a marriage in Nainital, and culminating in the swamplands of the Yamuna floodplains. 'Mein yahan Indira kaand ke time mein aaya.' I came here at the time of Indira's assassination. This is a peculiarity one encounters often in Buland Masjid. It was not any distress that caused him to flee to Delhi in 1984, during the mass killing of Sikhs after Indira Gandhi's assassination. It is just how he remembers the year, an oft-repeated measure of time among the people here. 'It was the struggle to survive and to earn that brought me here. I started off in Khari Baoli, selling dry fruits. When that failed, a friend introduced me to the firewood and coal business.' Yet, after decades of struggle he still lives in a state of visible poverty. You can only be astonished by his equanimity and good humour.

> Attar travelled through all the seven cities of love
> While I am only at the bend of the first alley.[20]

On a pavement, a small green felt carpet, a little pile of silken green swathes of cloth. Above, atop a tall wooden joist post, a green flag. Something makes you stop and take a longer look. Encased within this greenness is a little man on a small takth, his head swathed in a green turban. Reclining slightly, his legs stretched out before him, he holds a wooden staff in one hand. Alongside him, on the green felt, lies a dog, deep in slumber. I cannot help be fascinated by the theatrical incongruity. Who is this?

'I am Haré Baba.'

The Ghausia Masjid and mazaar stands away, a little separated from the cluster of Buland Masjid. A space of simplicity, a lone onion-domed structure of beauty. Today, money has transformed it into an unfinished confusion of brick and mortar. There were ambitious plans to build an elaborate new structure, and the mazaars of the five pirs, who were interred within the grounds of the old masjid, were to be shifted there. Halfway through, the money ran out. But here in this hidden corner, is the exemplar, the remnants of that sacred construct which bound the divinity of Islam within a loosely woven fabric that made space for a different way of being. I hear the melodious chorus of an energetic qawwali. They are celebrating the Urs of Syed Jalaluddin, the principal pir of Ghausia Masjid. On the way to the mazaar, one is assailed by a different music, which almost drowns out the sound of the qawwali. I look around to see where the sound is coming from. It is puzzling, annoying. I look up. In the dry dusty trees that line the walls of the graveyard are hundreds of swallows. Those little birds, once ubiquitous in the city, rarely seen today, are clustered here, in this environment of waste and degradation, their secret place of survival.

The eccentric wisdom of the Sufi faith, its dervish intoxication, its poetry, its music, the essential kindness of it, lends itself to a life of poverty that can be conducted with a semblance of dignity.

Haré Baba, like the wandering Sufi, had his own share of travails which saw him leave Calcutta in search of a better life in Delhi. Starting out as a labourer, his hard work mixed with chance and good fortune, he found himself established in Chandni Chowk, the owner of a flourishing jewellery business. But there was a tragic reversal of fate. 'Indira kaand ke time mein meri dukan mein chori hui aur sab khatam hogaya. Mein barbad hogaya.' At the time of Indira's assassination, my shop was robbed and I lost everything. I was ruined.

The trauma of that devastating loss persists. He begins to shake, his hands tremble. He puts up a hand as if to fend off the pain. 'Stop, please. I can't bear it, just wait awhile.' I sit with him, silent, not knowing what to do or say, how to comfort him. After a while, he regains his composure. It is difficult to continue, but he does. 'You see, what happened then was that I completely lost my mind—I spent days wandering the city, aimless, a madman.'

The madness of despair and the divine madness of the Sufi. Perhaps it was only fitting that he found comfort and refuge in his reinvention of himself as a wanderer of the faith. 'I embraced the faith and I am now a "Baba". I spend my time in contemplation of the Lord. I travel every Friday to Ajmer to offer prayers at the revered shrine of Moinuddin Chisti.' He spends the rest of his time accepting alms in return for guidance to troubled souls. 'I am at peace now. I have my faithful dog with me, he accompanies me everywhere. I have my wife and my seven children. By God's grace, we have enough to eat and live.' His poverty is evident, yet ironically so is his sense of contentment, a man at peace with himself.

The municipal school lies separated from the colony by an open field, the malodourous flattened remains of the landfill. When you leave after a brief interaction with the school authorities, you carry away the sense of despondency that hangs over this relatively new concrete structure, built by the government. It is when you encounter such despondency that you are nudged back into the heart of the darkness of India, divided worlds, everywhere here are glimpses into the depth of that gaping wound. Each is 'the other', separated by the rippling fault-lines of belief, culture, the long festering wounds of history. Here, within this secular edifice of the idea of India, you get a hint of the communal bloodlines that run across this country.

The principal I spoke to was a gentle, kindly man. His colleagues viewed my camera and me with suspicion, a sense of apprehension. They limited their responses to monosyllables. Suddenly a high-pitched verbal battle breaks out between two women outside the office. We cannot hear each other through this ruckus. Suddenly the women barge in uninvited, each dragging a young boy behind her. The boys are surly, sullen, staring accusingly at each other. One has tear-stained cheeks. The women begin venting their ire at the Principal. Apparently, there was a scuffle between the boys and the one at the receiving end promptly made a call to his mother, weeping copiously. The distraught woman charged into the classroom and, disregarding the teacher, delivered a stinging slap to the other boy. Now it was the turn of the other mother to land up, resulting in an angry exchange of words conducted at a disturbing volume. This exchange continued in the Principal's office and several attempts to calm them came to no end. Finally, they were persuaded to register their grievance with another school functionary. The beleaguered gentleman continues, almost apologetic for the conduct of the women: 'We deal with this on a regular basis. There is such tremendous indulgence of their children in this place, they will suffer no criticism against them. This is very sad, because these children are intelligent, bright, but very bereft of discipline. The result is, we have a very high dropout rate. As it is, the girls are pulled out early to help in domestic chores and often to make way for the education of their younger male siblings. But I am always heartened by their desire to educate their children.

'Things are made harder for them as the main medium of instruction is not Urdu, but Hindi. As a result, many leave to study in the local madrasas. Still, we persevere, many of our youngsters are doing very well.

'The problem is getting teachers to stay here. As soon as they are assigned to Buland Masjid, they want to get out as soon as possible. Most of them belong to Haryana, and being here begins to affect their sensibilities. Many look to bolt at the earliest opportunity.'

Once again, the pressures and difficulties of having to transcend cultural and social differences. A man from Haryana, a Hindu bound by a strict Arya Samaji vegetarian faith, would find himself fairly out of sorts in this environment. 'Look around,' and now his air of hope slowly dissipates, 'yahan ka jo mahaul hai, aap samajh sakte ho, yeh cheel-kauwe, yeh maas . . . ' You can understand, the milieu here, these kites, these crows, all this flesh . . . He waves towards the emptiness of the field outside, circled by kites, their predatory whistles echoing into the skies, as they swoop down, winging off with bits of pink flesh hanging out of their beaks. He drifts off into silence.

I had encountered a similar air of despondency almost two decades earlier. A little distance away from this colony was a police camp. The officer-in-charge bore the same mien—of a man defeated in his task of managing law and order within such environs of degradation. The man, tired not by his exertions, but out of sheer boredom at his desk. He toyed with a marbleized paperweight, rolled it around his table, his eyes following it. 'You see, there is not much we can do. Most of East Delhi is full of criminals from all parts of Uttar Pradesh who find refuge here. Totally criminal,' he repeated, not looking at me while he spoke, one hand now cradling his head, the other slicing an arc across the room.

Fortunately, at the local thana, there is no place for despondency. Constables come and go, there is the constant rumble of their motorcycles. The Station House Officer is a bit of a local legend, working hard to knit together disparate communities. Since his arrival, crime rates have gone down. 'In any case, most of the crime here is petty theft, small scale drugs and such like ... Of course, there are a few serious crimes, but basically the migrant wants to move on with life. Hunger and poverty are what he wants to fight, and, believe me, 98 per cent of the time, he will try to do this with honest hard work and labour.'

All dressed up and nowhere to go.
I coulda' been something.[21]

In an empty lot behind the colony, boys tear away at scraps of paper and stagger about with beatific smiles. I run into a boy I have met several times; he comes up to me, grins widely and proceeds to engage me in earnest chatter, repeating himself several times and dissolving into giggles. Further down, young boys sit on little piles of garbage as they rummage through the waste, their eyes darting half-lidded glances at me.

Every so often, walking around, you encounter such groups of boys, many of them in their stylish avatars, sniffing glue, peddling or being peddled drugs.

> I woke; my mind was bright with flame;
> I saw the cheap and sordid hole
> I live in, and my cares all came
> Burrowing back into my soul.[22]

> I live in shit
> My needle life a
> bruteist clock—
> it's always mid-day . . .
> the sky is rolling shadows
> all over the choking earth . . . [23]

Gun battles, cop-and-robber shoot-outs, ganglord killings, illegal smuggling of desi kattas, these are some of the more serious crimes that circle the environs of Buland Masjid.

Love, the moon, and murder, have poetry in them
by common consent.[24]

One day, watching *Once Upon a Time in Anatolia* (2011),
Nuri Bilge Ceylans' beautiful road movie cum crime
investigation, I am suddenly transported back to Buland
Masjid. The camera meanders through the visually stun-
ning landscape of the Anatolian countryside, gently
unfolding its narrative. A murderer is guiding the police
through the rolling hills, to recover the body of his victim.
I recall a news item:

> New Delhi [3 February 2012]. With the arrest of
> a 24-year-old man here, police today claimed to
> have solved a murder case in which the victim's
> head and torso were dumped in separate wells in
> Haryana's Mewat in 2006. Mohammed Arif, a
> resident of Buland Masjid in Shastri Park area
> was arrested from Farashkhana here yesterday on
> a tip-off [. . .] Arif told the police that he along
> with his friend had killed Abrar Ahmed, who had
> been residing in his neighbourhood and 'used to
> stalk' his sister. 'He had threatened Ahmed with
> dire consequences if he tried to meet his sister. He
> also got his sister married but Ahmed continued

to be friendly with her which annoyed the accused. Subsequently, he planned to eliminate Ahmed,' the official said. On December 6, 2006, he along with his cousin Shabbir went to Ahmed's house and lured him to come with them to Mewat on the pretext of meeting his sick grandfather, the police said. After reaching there, Arif killed Ahmed with the help of Shabbir using a butcher's knife and also severed his head. They threw Ahmed's torso and knife in a nearby well and dumped the head in another well, which was found by Haryana police the next day. [. . .] 'Arif pretended to be unaware about the incident and faked to help them in the search of the deceased,' he said.[25]

The life of Mohammad Zafar, who passed away in March 2016 at the age of 95, embodies the quintessence of survival, struggle and triumph. When an embankment project on the Ganges ended his fishing career in the Chambal village of Moradabad, more than a hundred miles away, he came to Delhi to take up fishing in the Yamuna: 'This was all swampland when I came here,' he recalled, 'We had no homes, just a sheet covering our heads. We transformed the land, with the sheer labour of our hands and somehow managed to erect tiny hutments.' In his lifetime, he saw more than three generations of his family establish themselves and thrive, eventually owning several houses across Buland Masjid. His extended family numbers more than 80, all living in Buland Masjid.

Zafar's story is exceptional in its sheer duration. But, in all other aspects, is repeated with variations by thousands of others who are pushed out of their homes, hundreds and even thousands of miles away, in rural areas or mofussil urban centres, and forced to seek their uncertain fortunes in Delhi.

Hunger. It was prevalent everywhere.[26]

If Buland Masjid was created as a paradise for the hopeless, the destitute, it has succeeded in becoming a paradise for the hungry. Food is everywhere, even to be stumbled upon in dark alleys.

In his *Parallel Lives*, Plutarch describes the Metoecia, or the Feast of Migration, a celebration of migrants leaving their boroughs and uniting in one city. Here in Buland Masjid, every day is a feast. The migrants have brought, with their rituals and traditions, memories of cuisines of their distant lands. Food is the connection that brings back the sense of the tender touch of love, hearth and home. Men haul carcasses, baste, cook. Dough is pounded vigorously. Rotis, naans, breads, tandoors. Bakeries turn out rusks and biscuits. Vendors crowd the narrow streets peddling strawberries, pastries; popcorn machines release the smell of warm butter; a man guides his cart outfitted with an unfathomable contraption which emits flaming sunbursts and rolls out perfectly formed nankhatais.

This is a gastronomical hub. Kiosks and tikka stalls abound, the atmosphere is laden with smoke and tempting aromas. Hunger prevails and so does food. The rituals of the cornucopia of plenty begin early. Barely has one ceased before the other commences. Kilos of white foaming milk are poured into an enormous kadhai in the early hours and stirred with a large ladle all day. Boys take turns to stir. In the evening, huge steel glasses of this mixture are enthusiastically consumed. The sensual aromatic of breads and meats mixes with the odours of offal and refuse, the gaseous releases from the open sewage drains.

But hunger still drives this dwelling of survivors.

On a particular day of wandering, in the dead of winter, with the acrid smoke, through a slight fog and mist, a wall, painted a pale sea green with a large mural. A painting of a rooster. The rooster, more than perhaps the masjid, is the appropriate symbol for this colony, where the main trade is one of the oldest in the world— the butcher's. Meat and the work of meat is the driving force of life in Buland Masjid.

There is a strange accommodation, a peaceful tolerance, a pact between all manner of animals. Goats, chickens, ducks and dogs, all in their own place, waiting, watching, and in the midst of it all, the rooster, crowing, calling, king of his world. And on a pale paint-washed wall, this fresco by an artist who went beyond his brief, to portray this symbol of survival.

The rooster becomes a symbol of fecundity, of courage, of prosperity, a homage to survival. In this place where beauty finds little space to flourish, an artist paints on his canvas in ambitious strokes. It is so alien, this artistic attempt, that it draws my imagination to a memory of another world, a memory so incongruous within this environment, of another pale paint-washed wall, far, far, away on the outer wall of a sacred monastery in the cold, dry desolation of the icy heights of Ladakh: the rooster rooted in the wheel of life depicted in Buddhist paintings. His symbolism in many other worlds. He announces the dawn and dispels the evil spirits of darkness. He is unlike the painted chicken at the dhaba in Ambala that proclaims, 'Meet me anywhere, but eat me at Deluxe dhaba.'

I ask after the artist, but no one can tell me anything, no one knew where he had gone. He came, painted this and left. One day, returning to the colony after a long break, I saw to my dismay that the mural had been erased. In its place was a new shiny cock, a flash paper poster, already torn at the edges.

The artist, and now his creation, were gone.

The life of a child in these squalid surroundings, deprived of light and space, would seem constrained, yet they seem at a joyous accommodation with their surroundings. A boy hurtles down the narrow road screaming at wayfarers to get out of his way. His feet are outfitted with a pair of smart red roller-skates. He is new to this art, and his face bears a mix of terror and wild delight as he rolls along, struggling to keep upright. He hits a pothole and barely escapes a crash, avoiding a bucket attached to rope which has been lowered from a tenement on the third floor. A man stands on the road, putting loaves of bread into the bucket, gives a tug to the rope and it is hauled up slowly. The boy survives and continues his careening down the road, now negotiating a cart filled with brightly coloured salwar suits, surrounded by excited young girls and women. In the heat of an August afternoon, he runs into a vendor on a cycle rigged up with bright festoons as he makes his way through, selling little versions of the tricolour.

You turn a corner and suddenly a small room stuffed with little boys, a few little girls and teenagers, a gaming room that would be well placed in a dystopian version of Star Wars. Their eyes locked on what are almost antiques, consoles discarded and bought in bulk by an enterprising gentleman who thought of the children of his colony. The boys jostle, push and stare transfixed as the lucky few manage to get to the controls and engage with these fascinating others worlds of exotic demons, villains, monsters and superheroes.

There are plenty of chance encounters that can arouse and illuminate a child's mind, pushing it to discover hitherto unknown, unseen, wonders.

Suddenly, one evening, hoardings, adorned with the strange form of a beautiful hippopotamus. His jaws wide open, drooling water and saliva. 'Daryayu Ghora!' River Horse, the hoarding proclaims, 'Pehli baar dekhiye!' For the first time. This fantastical image, so engaging, exotic.

A circus has come to town, lending an air of Coney Island to its surroundings. A brightly coloured tent sits in the middle of a clearing. Little boys in their kurta-pajamas and skull caps sit under the benign gaze of the huge hippopotamus that stares down at them from a large hoarding. A little away, within the precincts of the big top, the mighty beast awaits his evening meal. He emerges slowly, snout first, a pair of tiny eyes, little rounded ears, and then hauls his powerful giant body out of his generous water pool, and makes his way towards his feeding cage. The large crowd that has gathered to see this strange creature gasps as he sways past with an imperial gait, and watches in silence as he delicately picks his way through his lavish meal. A frisson of expectation, a sense of suspended anticipation, emanates from the crowd, contrasting sharply with the quietness of the gentle beast. He finishes his meal, slowly turns around and makes his way back, occasionally stopping to gaze at the crowd, before finally disappearing into the dark waters. Here in the middle of Shastri Park, this water-loving creature, so far from his native Africa. His presence stirs the languid imagination.

Buland Masjid does not lack the impetus for such flights of imagination. Another balmy afternoon, sleepy school children struggle to keep awake in class. Suddenly, looking out the window across the field, they see, to their astonishment, a graceful white flying craft gently float down into the playground. They rush out, screaming with delight. A microlight has made an emergency landing. For the children, this beautiful, engineered, delicate craft of flight is a marvel, an enchanting mechanical bird of paradise, here, on their grounds.

Adorning a terrace is a huge painting of a man in a top hat, black coat and bow tie, waving a wand: Shah the Magician. 'Come, learn magic tricks.'

Yes, within this world of poverty and squalor, there is a bit of magic that tweaks the human spirit, pushing it to seek the possibility of an existence beyond the mundane.

4

THE URBAN AGE

Gargantua went to see the sights of the town, and everyone stared at him in great wonder. For the Parisians are such simpletons, such gapers, and such feckless idiots that a buffoon, a peddler of indulgences, a mule with bells on its collar, or a fiddler at a crossroad will draw a greater crowd than a good preacher of the gospel.

The people so pestered him, in fact, that he was compelled to take a rest on the towers of the Notre Dame, and when from there he saw so many pressing all around him, he said in a clear voice:

'I think these clodhoppers want me to pay for my kind reception and offer them a *solatium*. They are quite justified, and I am going to give them some wine, to buy my welcome. But only in sport, *par ris*.'

Then, with a smile, he undid his magnificent codpiece and, bringing out his john thomas, pissed on them so fiercely that he drowned two hundred and sixty thousand, four hundred and eighteen persons, not counting the women and small children.

A number of them, however, were quick enough on their feet to escape this piss flood, and when they reached the top of the hill above the university, sweating, coughing, spitting and out of breath, they began to swear and curse, some in a fury and others in sport (*par ris*). 'Carymary, Carymara! My holy tart, we've been drenched in sport! We've been drenched *par ris*.'

Hence it was that the city was ever afterward called Paris.[27]

Buland Masjid is an accretion of filth, an old landfill that has now become home.

The landfill has slowly eaten its way into the Yamuna's fertile mud, looking almost innocuous in the heaps that it now forms. These piles of refuse are still set alight, their noxiousness scouring through the cilia. In the white heat of summer, sweat emits the slightly pungent whiff of shit and acid. Winter sees people coughing, lungs seeking to escape their cages, spewing out boluses, lumps of clogged mucus, dispatched with the ease of much practice.

Everywhere, people lounge about in this environment, forced to make their peace with it. They have taught themselves to endure. If no one will help them, they will help themselves. They will take this dump, scrounge within the festering toxicity of their fields and turn it into gold.

To start with, there is waste, scrap, the gold of the urban poor. In his book *History of Shit* (1978), Dominique Laporte sees the city as a 'jewel fed by lowly operations'. 'Whether belly or granary, the city is that place where merchandise accumulates and is consumed before being turned into gold.'[28]

Baudelaire writes of the ragpicker, 'He collates the annals of intemperance, the capernaum of waste. He . . . collects like a miser guarding a treasure, refuse which will assume the shape of useful or gratifying objects between the jaws of the goddess of industry.'[29]

Each rabbit hole is remaking, banging, crashing, welding, refashioning objects of discard, into something of reuse, utility.

These new cities within cities draw intricate webs of judicious industry. So Buland Masjid has a choice of pickings from the cluster of cities nearby. Today, there are several options available, little enterprises of industry among which the making and assembling of jeans is of the highest value. There is a frenetic movement of cycle rick-shaws overloaded with teetering bundles of jeans. Little pieces of blue clog drains. Tiny rooms are outfitted with state-of-the-art industrial cutting and sewing machines. Within minutes, swathes of blue are marked, cut, sewn, and behold, a swank pair of jeans is assembled. Labels are attached, and soon this item of clothing produced in Buland Masjid will adorn some of the swishest bottoms swaying along the promenades of wealth and privilege. All this done with an eye on the door. There is a sense of distracted energy, of haste.

And that mix of success and fear is the essence, the smell, that emerges from these cities. For all these worlds they have created out of nothing, these self-conjured worlds of enterprise and industry, lie within the ambit of that Damocles sword contained in one word: illegal.

Behind the scrap dealings, the bakeries, the jean junctions, the endless activities that feed the cities endless wants is the naked playing out of what drives the world— the creation of wealth, of urban conglomerates.

An economy of money starts from where once there was nothing, first bare land, then men, women and children, then houses. Once this captive unit establishes itself on the backs of the sheer labour and fatigue of thousands, then—they begin to straggle in—the politicians, the policemen and the laws.

This is the great 'urban century'. The complex bind of distress migration and urbanization is an ever-unfolding drama.

> Cities—in spite of their stagnant or negative economic growth—have simply harvested this world agrarian crisis. Peasants had no choice but to become urban.[30]

Buland Masjid is just one of the 1,797 'unauthorized' cities or, as is officially known, 'colonies' of Delhi.[31] These are a curious phenomenon, so at odds with the great idea of urban India and the 'smart cities' so meticulously being planned for this great urban age. What aspect of planning fits in with the total collapse of an agrarian economy and urban economies that have no machinery to absorb and support that phenomenal fallout? What vision of justice can reconcile with the reality and degradation of the thousands of Buland Masjids across India?

The incoherence of urban planning and the resultant tragedy reflects a colossal planning failure by those in charge. The ghettos of Delhi are nothing but a consequence of a series of active policy errors.

In 2011, despite pressing problems with a population of just over 13.8 million, the Delhi Development Authority's masterplan envisaged 'a balanced regional development' and the 'comfortable adjustment' of 23 million by 2021. A potpourri of ill-conceived projections, including some that were disastrously inaccurate, now fully exposed, 'Master Plan for Delhi 2021' put the estimate of 'urbanizable land' in Delhi at 97,790.9 hectares, and separately stated that 45 to 55 per cent of it—that is, 53,785 hectares at 55 per cent—was for residential use. It also sought a density of 225 persons per hectare of housing.[32] Simple multiplication would bring this figure to just 12.1 million—and not the targeted 22 to 23 million that the plan envisaged. A population of 22 million would take the density up to 409 persons per hectare. Even if 20 per cent of these were located outside the National Capital Territory (NCT) as the masterplan somewhat improbably envisaged, the density would still stand at 327. Population trends have already consigned all these numbers to the dustbin. Delhi's population was estimated at 29.4 million by 2019, rising to 31.18 million in 2021,[33] yielding a density of 539.59 per hectare of land for residential use.[34]

These were not honest errors of calculation, but intentional obfuscations, as were the masterplan's projections for housing. In 1961, the DDA was handed over 19,190 hectares for residential development,[35] but, till 2011, had not been able to build houses on even half that land. By 1968, a review of the housing situation revealed a shortage of 350,000 units. Till that year, a total of only 12,000 plots and 1,350 dwelling units had been made available.[36] In 2005, official figures placed the housing shortage at 400,000 units. By 2020, the shortage is estimated to have swelled to 2 million units.[37]

Far from a coherent approach to addressing this crisis, the DDA explicitly chooses to transform Delhi into a city of slums. The masterplan for 2021 baldly states that the existing slums will stay and will, in fact, be 'regularized'—a projection gradually being translated into reality through the political process. At least 3.6 million people lived in slums and jhuggi-jhopri colonies in Delhi[38] when the masterplan observed, 'the present three-fold strategy of relocation, in-situ upgradation and environmental upgradation' is good enough for these and must continue. Not a single slum—upgraded or otherwise—is fit for human habitation, and certainly not within the much-vaunted 'world-class city' which Delhi aspires to be.

DDA has comprehensively failed to create the housing and infrastructure for which it had acquired thousands of acres of land from farmers and private owners, and it is left to a desperate populace to scrape together 'dwelling units' on vacant lots. They are forced to break the law and to become squatters by the criminal inefficiency of state agencies. The result is that more than half the population of Delhi lives in 'illegal, makeshift' and unplanned shelters, which are, by and by, 'regularized', creating self-inflicted chaos. The notion of planning holds no meaning in such a scenario. By 2019, 1,797 unauthorized colonies had come up on public or private land without any approved layout or building plans.[39] An estimated 4 million people were living in these neighbourhoods, built over 43,000 acres.[40]

IF WE DON'T MIGRATE,
WE WILL STARVE TO DEATH HERE

Every day hundreds of people from these flood-prone areas of north Bihar districts [. . .] migrate to cities like Delhi, Gurugram and Ludhiana in search of their livelihood. [. . .] 'They are forced to leave their children, old parents and wives at home waiting for their monthly remittance to come.' [. . .] According to an estimate, around 45 lakh youths migrate from Bihar every year to make a living. [. . .] 'Most of the passengers reach the platform a day before to board the train and get a seat in the compartment.' [. . .] 'It doesn't matter if death awaits us in the cities . . . if we don't not migrate, we will starve to death here. We have no option but to catch this train to eke out a living for ourselves and our families,' says Mohd. Shagir from Nariyar village, before he goes back to digging the graves again.[41]

The fallout has been predictable: hundreds of millions of new urbanites must further subdivide the peripheral economic niches of personal service, casual labour, street-vending, rag-picking, begging and crime.[42]

The sheer scale and hideousness of corruption hidden in the inertia of government after government and their failure to create cities for the people. What are these 'world-class cities' we keep talking about? Someone wants to build flyovers, another wants to build a new Parliament, waste precious public money on destroying meticulously laid out, planned-to-the-last-aesthetic-detail monumental vistas. Indulgent, wasteful spending spreads itself with a wantonness across Delhi, demonstrating so amply the inability to imagine a functioning city, forget planning a great one. Unimaginative works showcasing a complete banality of aesthetic expression, derivative designs imported from outdated commonalities of the West, the Signature Bridge, a silly festoon, made with a criminal splurge of public funds; the new buildings of Pragati Maidan, even sadder in their architectural vocabulary than the rundown concrete PWD guesthouses in mofussil towns.

A bridge was needed; a good sturdy expansive one, could have been built. Yet what we have is a lurid vulgarity built at a cost of over 2,000 crore rupees over a period of 15 years, creating hell for the city.

'Beauty, cleanliness and order,' he famously said, 'clearly occupy a peculiar position among the requirements of civilization.'[43] The writhing chaos of 'the Delhis' would have surely driven Freud to a fecund analysis. Sadly, one does not have to resort to a Freudian imagination to see what ails this city. But the emperors gad about naked, shit does not smell. Just beyond the periphery of the many works of wasteful, indulgent splurging, lie the cities of the East, hoping that someone would look their way and throw them a buck of their own hard-earned money.

An International Labour Organization researcher has estimated that the formal housing markets in the Third World rarely supply more than 20 percent of new housing stock; out of necessity, people turn to self-built shanties, informal rentals, pirate subdivisions, or the sidewalks.[44]

Mike Davis, fuming forth on the politics of urbanization, predicts grim doomsday scenarios upon all our cities. He estimates that there are already some 200,000 such slums worldwide. The slum is becoming the blueprint for cities of the future, which, 'rather than being made out of glass and steel as envisioned by earlier generations of urbanists, are instead largely constructed out of crude brick, straw, recycled plastic, cement blocks and scrap wood.'[45]

But no one will do anything in a country that always rewards criminality. These ghettos of impoverishment become tools in the hands of governing elites, favourite hunting grounds during flashpoints of political credulity, or of disaster.

The illegality of the squatter and his extreme vulnerability, despite the security of this world that he has created for himself, leaves him at the mercy of these unscrupulous 'harbingers of justice'. This is where men like Maqsood begin their fight to oppose the stain of criminality thrust upon them by this ironic twist of selective justice. Everything hinges on a struggle to become 'legal' and retain their humanity. It is the powerless thousands, pitted against the power of the ten or so men who decide their fate, or destiny. In one stroke, they can all be herded out and be deprived of their means of sustenance, which they have laboured so industriously to create. Or, if fortune favours, then the magic words of 'legalized', 'authorized', will be flung at them, with the hope and the promise of uncertain future deliverance.

But within this construct of 'legality', the politician holds the vital key to empowerment; he holds the migrants' vote. They become a 'bank' of humans, to be exploited in the tussle to gain access to, and strut within, the corridors of power not too far away.

Or, suddenly, this land that they have made habitable is coveted by government agencies. These agencies decide, after decades, that they would like their land back, please. When they are met with a refusal, extreme, often cruel, methods are adopted to accelerate eviction.

In some other countries, there are tried-and-tested methods of freeing land from 'squatters'.

Rather than bear the expense of court procedures or endure the wait for an official demolition order, landlords and developers frequently prefer the simplicity of arson. Manila has a particularly notorious reputation for suspicious slum fires, especially in areas targeted for industrial development. Urban sociologist Erhard Berner describes a favourite method of Filipino landlords:

to chase a 'kerosene-drenched burning live rat or cat—dogs die too fast—into an annoying settlement . . . The unlucky animal can set plenty of shanties aflame before it dies.'[46]

Thus, we make our New Oxford Streets, and our other new streets, never heeding, never asking, where the wretches whom we clear out, crowd.[47]

While once slums shocked, today they are lauded for being places of industry. Here we have done away with all pretence of seeing the slum as a place that no living being should have to endure, let alone live in. Today, in this epoch which will perhaps be looked at as one of the greatest ages of man for the advances in the sciences and the astounding breakthroughs, the millennial leaps in technology, we find that inequalities, poverty and ignorance abound. This is the horrific irony of our age.

Untold-of wealth is being created but its spread, its dispersion, remains tightly controlled. There is not much to applaud here. To present these as centres of industry is so wrong, so fallacious a narrative, spun by those who reap the benefits of these suffering toilers, for their own selfish purposes, aggrandizement and prosperity. The lyrical paeans are sung by those from outside, looking in.

5

A RETURN

What aspiration can now arise from this place of arrival? There is food here. Men are now free to think. There are networks here, and it is in a man's fate into which of these he will be drawn.

In the frenetic cycles of the day, enacting the bit-by-bit chores that eventually create the life it feeds off, Buland Masjid is never far from the idea of the political. Politics is everywhere, yet nowhere. Almost all the walls are adorned with posters of men who operate within the rungs of politics. Poster is stuck upon poster, creating unique, inadvertent collages. An old man, beautiful in his crinkled visage, his eyes twinkling, comes to me, 'Take my picture,' he says. Later that evening as I look through the photographs, I see his grin, his one long tooth, a face brimming with a kindly delight and, in an enchanting stroke of serendipity, the words 'Lovely-ji' plastered on the wall behind him. They are leftover scraps of a poster of Arvinder Singh Lovely. The Congress Party politician haunts Buland Masjid with his ubiquity. He pops up in a decrepit piss-filled alley, grinning benignly at you, his face a full-cheeked, shiny reckoning of the pop singer Daler Mehndi.

A small, glossy new garment showroom has brought in four square-jawed male mannequins and adorned them in the razzle of their offerings, their outstretched arms holding aloft shawls and scarves. They startle you, these men outfitted in silks and satins. Just above them is a hoarding proclaiming 'Aam Aadmi Party'. The juxtaposition of these mannequins and the hoarding ironically outline the absence of these politicians.

Rizwan Bijnori is a delightful, canny gentleman who runs me through the anecdotal fortunes of Buland Masjid. I meet him while in conversation with Dr Ishtiaq, who has an Unani clinic in the colony. Also present at the clinic, which doubles as a mini adda where friends stop by and catch up with the doctor, is Sohan Lal, an old and close friend and one of the few Hindus in the colony. His story is no different from the others, 'I came here looking for a life.' As a Hindu, was it not odd to settle in a colony that was primarily Muslim? 'I don't know, I never saw it that way. A friend brought me here and I have been here ever since. My life, my friends, my family, they are all here. This is the only place I have known.' After the initial mandatory labour, he had enough to buy an inexpensive camera. 'It was difficult in the beginning. I would take photographs of the local leaders or VIPs when they would visit. Then I began to shoot portraits of people from the colony. Slowly I built up my trade, and was successful in setting up a little studio for myself.' Meanwhile, Rizwan is engaged in a jocular verbal joust with the doctor, and the latter is at the losing end, 'Main inko kehta rehta hoon, ye Barelvi hum Bijnorion se kabhi nahin jeetenge.'—I keep telling him, you Bijnoris will never win against us Barelvis.

'Aap mere dhabe pe aayein thein'—You had visited my dhaba—Bijnori reminds me and, pointing to Sohan Lal and the doctor, adds, 'Hamara bahut purana mel hai'—We share a very old relationship. So, what is this superiority of the Bijnoris, I ask in jest. 'You see,' the doctor interrupts, 'these Bijnoris can never stop talking!'

Watching and listening to this camaraderie, I sense the warmth, but also an underlying subtext that I cannot immediately grasp. 'Well,' Rizwan says, 'most of us are here from various parts of UP. We have the Barelvis, people from Shahjahanpur, Bijnor, Moradabad, Badaun, we also have migrants from Bihar, Bengal. But,' he hastens to add, 'we have no differences as such.' Slowly, out of nowhere, a community has formed, a band of brothers, and within it the intricate, convoluted complexities that dog the dark interiors of society across India. Everything is divided, subdivided, castes within castes, gotras, beliefs, practices, speech, linguistics, customs, mores, the list is endless. Even within close cultures, with the good-natured barbs and droll jesting, there is a tinge of abrasiveness. Here, within this narrow band of communities, largely from Uttar Pradesh, you get a foot-in-the-doorway glimpse of these divisions.

Within these eight and a half acres are six mosques. In this colony peopled by those largely of the Sunni sect, some follow the Deobandi and others the Barelevi persuasion. Faith and the strict practice of it, is followed with a dedicated devotion. Every namaz, every call to prayer, is a summons that meets with ready compliance.

But it is the modern god of wealth that dominates and dictates all fortunes here. Money is the god of Delhi.

After the creation of a certain security and prosperity, there is the question: what next? Besides the guidance of faith and the laws of the book, men are often at a loss; the creation of a secular temper, of interactions and ideas of other worlds, scarcely reach this enclosed city. The aspirational desires can only feed on the secular vulgarities of television, mainstream Bollywood films and the addictive titillations of contemporary social media.

As Rizwan Bijnori puts it, 'Our children can only dress up, badger their fathers and indulgent mothers for motorcycles and fancy clothes, phones, and just spend the day wastefully darting around the colony. There is not much more that this colony can offer. People are left to their own resources. Those who have the time and the means to think of anything beyond, rarely manage to step into the world of ideas, of the accomplishments of the mind.'

On the drive to Bijnor, a good road, the river Ganges, and suddenly small towns that appear like larger Buland Masjids. The same people, the same faces go past. A turn off the main road and then an 8-kilometre drive. Fields of sugarcane line the road. Rizwan has invited me to visit his village. 'I hardly go there now, but you must come and see my home.'

He waits for me at the turn-off. We follow his car, a red Maruti Swift, down the bumpy road. Sugarcane trembles in the intense cold—thin dry reeds, swaying in the breeze. A slow warmth creeps into the car, along with the smoky aroma of melted molasses. A little further down the air is filled with sticky smoke. Huge vats, in pits dug into the field, are being filled with the beautiful steaming amber of melted molasses. Men stir the vats—golden-orange pools of deliciousness—with huge ladles.

This age-old ritual transforms the banality of the fields. I get out of the car. Rizwan stops too, and from his car pour out an astonishing number of gentlemen, each distinct in character and deportment. They are the village elders, the notables, the welcoming committee accompanying Rizwan. They wait patiently as I take photographs.

When we finally arrive at his village, I am overwhelmed by the outpouring of warmth and goodwill. Rizwan has pulled out all the stops. The village itself is a surprise, clean, with pucca roads and proper concrete houses painted in vivid shades of green, blue or yellow. Rizwan has been sending money home for years and the family has created a large spacious house divided between the brothers. As I sit in his courtyard, I am joined by the village pradhan and the local schoolteacher. This is a relatively less deprived area of the vast Uttar Pradesh backwaters. After the initial pleasantries, tea and snacks, they slowly draw a picture of the lives of men far from Delhi. In no time, they are elaborating on the tragic economy of sugar and sugar cane, the single largest industry here. I am aghast at the appalling idiocy of a chronically distressed economy, a jumble of skewed, opportunistic transactions, naked and shameful in their exploitation of the farmer. Despite being in an affluent part of the state, such practices have made this a difficult place to live in, with only the most rudimentary facilities for health, primary education and welfare.

If Rizwan's and other houses are pucca and well built, it is because of the returning bounty of the city, of Buland Masjid. He takes me for a walk around the village. We pass another house, a strange structure, its courtyard sunk into the earth, and two modest thatch-roofed, earthen-walled rooms. A young girl sits cross legged on a rope charpai next to her mother. A couple of goats are tied in a corner. The place is scrupulously clean, but it is also the bare bones of a habitation. The girl is quietly rolling tobacco leaves into beedis. After introducing me, Rizwan moves me along. I say my goodbyes, nodding and smiling. It was an awkward and shy moment. She is a widow, he tells me, and had three young girls to bring up. They were now all of 'marriageable' age. The village panchayat tries to help out, getting them the odd job, such as beedi rolling and other work which can be done from home. The stark poverty of the family stands out against the more fortunate structures that have been embellished by the migrant economy.

The village itself, the landscape is almost sylvan. The mandatory pond retains its original health and beauty. The waters are clean, the pond is full. Large trees surround it, trees growing from times before Rizwan. A huge palm tree stands isolated on another bank, reflecting its fronded splendour in the rippling waters. Beyond, a couple of old havelis survive, with their sympathetic architecture of arches and pillared verandas, so suited to the weather and natural contours of these flatlands. The bulk of the village cuts a horseshoe layout around the pond, leaving one side free of habitation. The muezzin's call lilts across, a poetic edict, echoing its ancient cry. 'This is so beautiful,' I tell him. 'Yes, it is,' he says. After a pause, he adds a little wryly, 'but it cannot sustain us.'

———

The sadness of the return economy is that it leaves people with money but, as in Buland Masjid, with nothing to spend it gainfully on. There is the same import of style and swagger, but without any opportunities to engage in, let alone choose from. Money is thrown back, a little goes a long way in rural India, people build mini-palaces, mosques, temples, buy cars, a lot of the glitz of urban consumerism makes its way there, but a way of life—buffaloes and men in the same house, each lost in his cycle of fate—continues. No industry or enterprise that could create a sustainable economy comes in with this transfer of money. As a result, the village remains unable to sustain the returning migrant. Wealth without ideas of the mind that draw from the best the world has to offer. The positive aspects of raising a people out of poverty, out of hell, spreading equity and acting as a social leveller, are negated. There is a blowback against this very aspirational equality. Entrenched social divisions do not lend themselves to overnight rightings.

Migrant Mother. It was one of the most iconic images of the great depression. Dorothea Lange's photograph of the young woman, her weary face, mouth pulled downwards, eyes squinting into the distance, disinterested in the invasive gaze of the camera, her mind on the business of existing, of hunger, of living. Her children are burrowing close to her, their faces turned away, as if clutching her for protection. In her arms, she cradles an infant. Lange wrote in her notes:

I did not ask her name or her history. She told me
her age, that she was 32. She said that [she and
her children] had been living on frozen vegetables
from the surrounding fields, and birds that the
children killed. She had just sold the tires from her
car to buy food.[48]

Lange titled the photograph: *Destitute pea pickers in California. Mother of seven children. Age thirty-two. Nipomo, California.*[49]

Years later, Florence Owens Thompson, the woman in the photograph, was asked by a reporter how she had survived those years of struggle. She spoke plainly, with no sentimentality. 'We just existed,' she said. 'Anyway, we lived. We survived, let's put it that way.'[50]

'We never had a lot,' said Katherine McIntosh, her daughter, 'but she always made sure we had something. She didn't eat sometimes, but she made sure us children ate.'[51]

6

AND THEE BY MY SIDE: THE GOOD WOMEN

Women are to be seen everywhere, but their stories, narratives, get overwritten in the tales of triumph and survival. Or are they? The women appear to submit to their men, preferring to watch, to listen. After a while in Buland Masjid, I began to discover that there was something beyond this silence, something else. These women may not be speaking, they were always in the background, but there was an impression that within those women was steel.

This was quite unlike anything I had encountered before. The men, all of those I met and spoke to at length, seemed to defer to the women, look at them, nod towards them. They were not passive spectators, they were the strength, the determination, and crucially, they were partners. The role of the women in these stories of migration followed a similar articulation echoed everywhere. It is because of her, if she was not there, she was the only one who helped . . . Again and again, the men seem to reiterate: 'she'. Yes, Buland Masjid is the edifice created by the migrants and its steel frame, their women.

Despite the prevalence of severe orthodoxy, it is as if extreme adversity had helped them break through that straightjacket. Men seemed to need to keep looking over their shoulders to see this pillar of support, 'Yes, you can do it. Keep going.'

In the home of 95-year-old Zafar, grumbling through his story at everyone around him, yet unable to hide his pleasure in the telling of it. His wife, tiny, frail, stands beside him, hand on his shoulder, gently encouraging him to continue. Her eyes are brimming over with a mix of pride and never-to-be-forgotten pain. She intervenes once to address me directly. Softly she says, 'Bahut mushkil tha.'—It was extremely difficult—and lapses back into silence. He reaches out and, without looking at her, touches her hand. His body heaves with the effort. Holding her hand, the man who has lived to see more than three generations born, live and settle here, gently caresses that worn-out embodiment of support that rests on his shoulder. 'Agar yeh nahin thi toh mujh se kuch nahin hota'—If she had not come into my life, it would never have been possible for me to have done anything—he rasps out through halting breaths. It is a moment of such beauty, this ravaged bond that survived the long, long walk and the arrival.

I recall Maqsood's face as he showed me his wedding photograph. I recall his wife, sitting on the bed, listening. I remember his vast sense of gratitude towards her, his face suffused with warmth and pride. She was the one whom he turned to every time he was caught in a bind. He spoke of her as an equal or perhaps more. I remember her words, her quiet dignity: 'There is nothing extraordinary in what we did. We had to survive. Once were able to sustain ourselves . . . No one chooses to live in filth. Even a bird will build its nest, a home for its family, and try to make it beautiful.'

At one corner of a fetid galli is a matchbox-sized tea shop. A middle-aged woman sits pouring out cups of tea for the odd customer. Krishna Devi's story unfolds through a chance discovery. In a corner of this colony of masjids, you catch sight of the conical dome of a temple. A tiny concrete structure painted dull pink. It is locked. Someone goes off to get the key. Krishna Devi appears, nods and smiles and unlocks the door. A temple in the middle of an almost exclusive Muslim colony is a bit of a shock. Who built this temple? To whom does it belong? 'Main-ne banaya hai.' I built it. This woman, quiet and innocuous, is transformed at that minute into a figure of determination, of power.

It is a small room, enough to hold two people. Inside is the statue of the goddess Vaishno Devi. The startling stare of her gaze holds you. Her long red tongue unfurled, a heady mix of fear and insouciance, of power, of destruction.

Vaishno Devi and Krishna Devi—two goddesses—one a divine manifestation, the other a mortal, mother earth.

She chose to start the narrative of her life from after her marriage. She did dwell on her childhood, her parents, her life as a young girl. Life began with her marriage and it was already tough. 'There was hunger. We had no food, no money. We realized that if we wanted to survive, we would have to leave, there was nothing for us in Gorakhpur, nothing that would allow us to live. We had a relative who had left for Delhi sometime earlier. Hearing of our plight, he told us to pack our bags and come to Delhi. We left our home for Delhi 40 years ago.

'But we found that Delhi was not easy. Yes, the streets were paved with gold, but it was very difficult for us to scrape together a life. My relative told us of this place, and we were able to get ourselves a jhuggi here. My husband worked as a labourer and I set up this tea stall. We had no children then, it was just the two of us.

'As Hindus, it never struck us that we were in a place dominated by Muslims. That sort of thing was never in anybody's mind. In fact, so many people helped out and eased our travails with their kindness.

'What sustained my husband and me was our complete faith and belief in Mata Vaishno Devi. We knew that, with her by our side, we would be able to endure any hardship and come through. There was no temple for worship here. We took a pledge that if we were able to have children and build ourselves a house, we would construct a temple devoted to her.'

The presence of the temple is evidence that the world that they had conceived, that little paradise they had dreamt of, was eventually realized.

But tragedy was to strike this little self-created paradise. 'All was going well when suddenly I lost my husband. His passing left me with four little children to bring up. But I did not weaken my resolve. In fact, if anything, my resolve was strengthened. I had to keep strong, more so because I now had four little ones to bring up. And I was going to try my hardest to give them the best life that was possible.'

I hear Maqsood's echo in this part of her narration. 'Shiksha—I understood if I had to help them realize their dreams, the only way possible was through a good education. I was going to give them the best education, never mind how hard I would have to work for it.'

All around, you encounter this burning desire to give their children the best in life. Though, for so many, it manifests as an uncertainty about what is the best. Unable to answer that adequately, they bring their children up with ruinous indulgence, splurging on clothes, gizmos or whatever takes their children's fancy. Krishna Devi's clear-mindedness is rare. Indeed, she is a rare woman.

'I took up odd jobs, I worked in people's houses and somehow managed to keep the tea shop running. With great effort, I managed to do what I wanted with the blessings of the Devi and the guidance of the spirit of my husband.'

But what this woman achieved was driven by her fierce determination to give her children a chance at life.

One of the terrible fates that can befall a human being is to be born intelligent or sensitive in an English slum. It is like a long, slow, exquisite torture devised by a sadistic deity from whose malevolent clutches escape is almost impossible.

Such was not always the case. My father was born in an English slum in the years before the First World War. In the borough in which he was born, one in every eight children died in his first year. But in those benighted times, when some London children, too poor to buy shoes, went to school barefoot, the 'vicious cycle of poverty' had yet to be discovered. It had not yet occurred to the rulers of the land that the circumstances of a person's birth should seal his destiny. And so, my father, having been found intelligent by his teachers, was taught Latin, French, German, mathematics, science, English literature, and history, as if he were fully capable of entry into the stream of higher civilization.

When he died, I found his school textbooks still among his possessions, and they were of a rigor and difficulty that would terrify a modern teacher, let alone child. But he, who was never generous in his praise of others and often imputed the worst of motives to his fellow beings, remembered his teachers with the deepest respect and affection: for they had not only taught him his lessons but had devoted much of their spare time to taking their intelligent slum children, himself included, to museums and concerts, to demonstrate to them that the life of the slum was not the only life there was. In this way, my father was awakened to the very possibility of possibility.[52]

The Indian slum has not awoken to the 'possibility of possibility'. The faltering, timorous efforts that bolster attempts at providing an educational framework fail to engage the imagination and attention of the young. It requires the intervention of exceptional inputs from parents to guide and shape the intellectual reserves of their children, or an exceptional understanding of nurturing the intellectual value that could help children leapfrog out of this world of bleakness.

And that is what Krishna Devi had, the basic understanding that 'I had to give them the best education possible.'

I meet her son Kanhaiya. He is the embodiment of Krishna Devi's struggle, her vision. 'I am doing my PhD in environmental sciences from Delhi University. I did my graduation and postgraduate degree from Kirori Mal College. I always had an interest and a curiosity that leaned towards the sciences. I am lucky that I was in a school that encouraged my scientific temper. My mamma,' that is how as he addresses her, 'refused to put me in the local school. She sent me to Ludlow Castle to study.'

Ludlow Castle is a school in the Civil Lines of Old Delhi. Once the residence of the Governor General, it was turned into a school after Independence.

'I was very lucky to have excellent teachers who nurtured my interests.' Kanhaiya continues to pursue his career in academics.

In 2019, Krishna Devi quietly left her past behind, the place from where it all began. She, with her daughter, and her boys, now successful men, engaged in a last communion with the place that was home to her inspiration, her goddess of light and guidance, and shut the temple doors one final time. The goddess moved to a new home, a new beginning. The migration continues, but with serenity accompanied with joy.

———•—

It is something you cannot miss, the red door. Adjoining the door is a glass frontage through which blonde bewigged busts of two female mannequins stand out. The mannequins, the red door, are a Daliesque stroke in a narrow galli. In this little city that abounds with salons and stylist parlours for men, outfitted with state-of-the art accoutrements, this is the only beauty parlour for women. Young women walk in unobtrusively, to get their eyebrows threaded, their hair bleached and facials, all of which are performed by the owner, Nafisa, and her daughters.

Nafisa has the mien of an astute business woman. 'One has to try to make as much money as one can. As it is, my husband keeps unwell, so I decided to start my own business. There is nowhere for women to go when they are getting togged up as brides, or for young women generally. So, I stepped in and set up this place.'

This little one-room set-up helped her marry three daughters into 'good' families. The marriage of girls is always a huge financial burden on parents. Nafisa with her sharpness and drive refused to get bogged down in the face of the financial crisis brought on by her husband's inability to work. She faced the challenge square on and succeeded, keeping her good humour intact. She now has ambitious plans of expanding her business and raising enough money to enable them to shift out of Buland Masjid. She has the confidence to look beyond. 'Iss jagah ne humein bahut diya hai, magar ab time aa gaya hai ke hum iss jagah se shift ho jayen. Idhar ka mahaul ab sahi nahi raha.' This place has given us a lot but now it is time to move on. The entire milieu here is very degraded. She looks forward to the day when she can move her family and her daughters' families out of here and onward, towards a new migration.

In a little clearing behind the school is a small space that turns into a popular eating joint. Tikka stalls are set up and men and women gather around. When I first came here, I was capturing this general festive atmosphere, the smoke and the bleeding yellow swirls of light from the large halogen lamp above, when suddenly my camera lens caught a face. It was a woman making tikkas. This was a rarity. So far, I had only seen men engaged in this activity. And that face, a face wrapped with a purple dupatta, a face that showed up on the viewfinder. The exquisite symmetry of a model, there she sat, without make up, simple, or simply beautiful. Her face, her occupation, engage my attention. How was she 'manning' a tikka stall? In the evening hours, women kept to their homes or stepped out only when accompanied or for routine domestic chores. And here she was, young, beautiful, asserting her independence. But her looks, I found out later, were quite deceptive. She was much older than she appeared to be.

Shabana came to Delhi just after her marriage. After her husband died, she found herself alone and unable to return to her village—there was nothing there that could support her and her young daughter.

This fine-boned woman sits there, holding her own in a man's world. Making kebabs is a skill she taught herself after she was left to fend for her family, a widow, at a very early age.

The years have been kind to her and, amazingly, her misfortunes and her struggle have not visibly marked her. I learn that her life has been extraordinarily harsh and lacking in any kind of support. She sustained herself, taking up jobs where she found them, working houses as a domestic help in Chandni Chowk and returning to set up her kebab stall in the evening. Through all this, she supported a daughter, married her, and was now supporting her daughter's family, including a granddaughter she dotes on.

It was, as she tells it, a very lonely and hard journey, 'But the love of my daughter, and the strength I derived from that love, gave me the courage to continue. And now I have a granddaughter who gives me joy.'

It seems to be a simple thing to have done, but running a kebab stall is almost uniquely a man's work because of the kind of clientele it tends to attract and the hours at which the business peaks. 'I knew I would have to do whatever I could, to give my daughter the best life possible. Even though it was difficult, all the pain was forgotten when I held my granddaughter for the first time.'

The gentle Pir Baksh found his mate, his partner, in the equally gentle Naseeba. Her eyes are bright and sharp, she is an intelligent woman. What is destiny? Was Pir Baksh her destiny? Is a woman's destiny her man, does she only get to follow the journey he takes? Is her life the walk, or the trudge alongside?

There is a sense of intimacy beyond the conventional bond of husband and wife, beyond the affection that develops between a couple that appreciates each other. The way they speak to each other, the way each looks at the other, is different. You can see them as having enjoyed their time together. Unlike the others, she does not stand back, supportive from a distance. There was in her, a spark, a sense of fun, of spunk. She was different.

Always with a ready smile, she has an ebullience, a radiance that shines out within the grubby interiors of Buland Masjid. I recall when I first met her, I mistook her to be Pir Baksh's daughter. 'No, no,' he hastily proclaimed, 'this is my wife, Naseeba.' There were two young girls sitting beyond the partition that divided the little room. 'Those are my students,' she explained. Was she a teacher? 'No, but I teach the children of the colony, I give them tuitions, this is just something I do on my own, I would never dream of charging a fee. I would like to help the children and this is my small contribution, my way of

doing so.' How many students did she have? 'About three–
four come in daily. Some days, I may get more.' I thought
of the earnings she could get by charging a fee. This was
something that went beyond mere generosity.

She had a good laugh and a chuckle when I told her
I wished to talk to her, know her story. 'What is there to
tell?' she asked with amusement. When I persisted, she
finally agreed. We would sit in the little half of the room,
the sun pouring in through the makeshift wooden shutter,
huge dust motes swimming in the golden shafts of light.
Sometimes Pir Baksh or Razida their daughter would join
us, listening to her, helping jog her memory.

The first bit of information she shares reiterates her
innate uniqueness. 'Actually, I used to keep a diary, jotting
down stuff about my life, my days, simple things. I'd
compose little poems, put them down, my thoughts . . . '
Once again, the ready laugh at my amazement. Would she
share the contents of her diary with me? 'It's been many
years, I don't know if I will be able to find it, but if you
insist, I will search for it.' Indeed, it had turned out, she
was different.

Unlike most of the other residents she does not belong
to a farming family. Naseeba's life began in the picturesque
environs of Nainital. 'What a world that was! So beautiful!
I was lucky to have been born in a place of such beauty.

My father was in the police, he was a constable. We were a large family. You are asking me now to recount those days, I can't tell you, it was such a long time ago, but the warmth, laughter, the love has remained with me. It was a joyous childhood.' Here she stops, she is still smiling, but her eyes are brimming with tears. Pir Baksh reaches out and holds her hand. 'It's nothing,' she says, trying to brush off her tears, 'it's just those memories . . . we were happy but we were very poor, very poor.' Pir Baksh looks at me with an air of concern, as he repeats her words, 'Very poor'. They sit holding hands, silent for a bit. Then she continues: 'There was barely anything to eat. Sometimes we would just have a cup of tea with a little gur in it. But my father sent all of us to school, he insisted on an education for us girls too.

'I loved going to school, I was an excellent student, I was given a scholarship. I was very good at sports too.'

As I listen to her, this woman here, in these surroundings, I wonder at chance, at fate. Her natural intelligence, her sense of curiosity, her sharp mind. Could they have taken her down another road? A migration towards another destination? 'Mein chahti thi ke mein apni studies complete karoon, mein teacher banna chahti thi.' I wanted to complete my studies, I wanted to become a teacher.

95

A common acquaintance, a 'muh-boli behen'—one regarded as a sister—arrives with a proposal, a marriage for the 16-year-old. 'Kyonke hum bahut garib the, mere father ne haan kar di. Unho-ne kaha, "Tum naseebon wali ho, ladki ko aise rishte nahin aate hain. Bahut dhoondne parte hain." 'Because we were very poor, my father accepted the proposal. He told me, 'You are very blessed, girls rarely get proposals like this.'

It was a cruel irony that the very gifts, the qualities, that had made her stand out as special, attracted a rishta for her. A Qazi, a veil, an acquiescence, and it was done— she was married; to a man she saw for the first time only after the wedding.

But, she says smiling shyly, I was lucky, he was a good man, I liked him. Shortly after the wedding, they came to Delhi. Pir Baksh was already established in Buland Masjid. 'This is where I was brought as a young bride and this is where I have been ever since. Jab main yahan pahunchi, mujhe jhatka laga. Kahan Nainital aur kahan Buland Masjid! Par mein-ne kaha: Koi baat nahin, ab yehi mera ghar hai, hum adjust karenge.' When I first arrived, I was shocked. From the sylvan beauty of Nainital to Buland Masjid! But I comforted myself and said: Never mind, this is our home now, I will adjust. It is afternoon, I join her as her students wrap up their lessons. She makes tea for all of us. I ask her if she has managed to find her diary. Sadly, she cannot locate it. 'But what I have managed to find, thanks to you, are some old photographs. I will share those with you.' The children leave. 'You see,' she says, 'this place is beset with a lot of problems, it is difficult to bring up children in this atmosphere. Earlier, things were not so bad, but nowadays, this scourge of drugs is really disturbing. That's why I try to help the children, try to keep their minds on studying, on learning things of value.'

What comes through is her sense of pride. She presents herself as an individual. 'I have always conducted myself on the principles that my father instilled in me, courage and discipline. He always taught me to face life square on. And that is what I have always tried to do.' With a quiet smile she tells me, 'Last night someone broke into our home and stole our goat. But I try to take such adversity on the chin. After the initial sense of anger and of despair, I am trying to put it out of my mind and just comfort my husband, who is distraught. I just hope they don't harm the goat and keep it for its milk like we used to.' The loss of the goat was huge . . . but it was a setback she was already putting behind her.

More than three decades spent in Buland Masjid, with just an annual visit home. Her home, a place where she was brought up with love, there was hunger, but love prevailed. And it was that love that made the journey with Naseeba. It was what she brought to Buland Masjid.

Behind every small success is etched an unspoken sorrow, matched equally with the will to survive, to prevail. From childhood, it is a journey marked by relentless difficulties, pushing against a system that allows no space for them. The big city remains outside their grasp. There is a force of exclusion that always pushes them back, confining them to their ghettos.

'The city we built.'
The creation of a thousand
migrants and more. A place of
filth and instability; a place of
joy and security.
The minarets—the
embodiment of divinity—
loom on the horizon.

This is, on first sight, a world of slums and squalor, where pigeonhole dwellings hold dark secrets close to their hearts.

Yet, what one encounters is a world of Almadovarian excess.

A new generation has been sheltered from the struggle for sheer survival that their fathers and grandfathers endured. Cossetted and indulged, they splurge on flashy bikes, follow the latest fads and trends. They dare to dream, stars in their eyes, their aspirations shaped by Bollywood fantasies. But dreams often die hard . . .

Saqib's father and grandfather were both in the butcher's trade. He is already divorced from those memories, and dreams of escaping the confines of the ghetto to Bollywood stardom, to follow in the footsteps of his idol, Salman Khan.

Pir Baksh's indomitable spirit has survived the long journey from Khurja to this eccentric little corner, where coal and goats and eggs jostle for space with his family of eight.

(FACING PAGE)
His radiant wife Naseeba and their daughter Razida have shared the journey with him.

Life, laughter and madness spill out into the maze of streets and gallis. There is tragedy here, and there is triumph.

7

ARRIVAL CITY

Darkness has dawned in the East
On the noon of time:
The death-birds descend to their feast,
From the hungry clime.
Let Freedom and Peace flee far
To a sunnier strand,
And follow Love's folding-star
To the Evening land![53]

Everywhere, on boats, trains, planes, they are fleeing. We are besieged by migrants. The Third World, the East, constantly knocking on the doors of the privileged West.

There is a painting by Pieter Bruegel the Elder, *Two Chained Monkeys* (1562)—its beauty conveys a sense of tragic poignance. Two collared mangabeys, an exotic species from the coastal area of West Africa, sit in an alcove. Behind them is an arched opening overlooking the port and the sea, the Antwerp harbour. One of them has his face turned away, huddled and bent, his arms folded tightly into his chest. He looks towards the sea, and the ships docked there. We see the face of the other, he appears bewildered but, on closer inspection, he seems more in a state of pondering reflection. His air of bewilderment comes from the white eyelids that are common to this particular species. Chain links from a thick iron ring are anchored to girdles around their waists. Discarded nutshells are scattered about. There is an air of captivity, of exhaustion, of hunger, a long voyage, suggestive of the Dutch conquests of the colonies. The exoticism of the monkeys suggests that they have arrived from one of the far-off lands, a forced migration. Bruegel must have seen these beautiful creatures, scared and cowering, offered as exotic exhibits on display. There was more to his painting than the mere portrayal of two beautiful monkeys against the background of the Antwerp harbour.

Europe's rapacious peregrinations across the world, those ungenerous excursions, the sun turns its clock and brings in its wake the millions shrouded in darkness, now streaming into the West.

In 2016, the Venice Architecture Biennale had a special theme, 'Reporting from the Front'. In response to this, the German exhibition 'Making Heimat. Germany, Arrival Country' offered a model of the Arrival City—a way of designing urban spaces as they adapt and accommodate migrants.[54]

Just how torn apart Germany would be as a result of the refugee question was not something the curators expected. After more than a million people arrived in Germany in 2015, the nation's landscape shifted. Since then, the political right has been strengthened, borders are going up again and the notion of a welcoming culture has become history.[55]

Xenophobia is the new cult of civilization.

Improvements in civilisation are real enough, but they come and go. While knowledge and invention may grow cumulatively and at an accelerating rate, advances in ethics and politics are erratic, discontinuous and easily lost. Amid the general drift, cycles can be discerned: peace and freedom alternate with war and tyranny, eras of increasing wealth with periods of economic collapse. Instead of becoming ever stronger and more widely spread, civilisation remains inherently fragile and regularly succumbs to barbarism. This view, which was taken for granted until sometime in the mid-18th century, is so threatening to modern hopes that it is now practically incomprehensible.[56]

Europe's bloody century of world wars defined its civilizational temper. In Roberto Rossellini's powerful film *Rome, Open City* (1945), Captain Hartmann declares in despair, in his confrontation with Major Bergmann:

> We can't get anywhere, but
> kill . . . kill
> We have sown Europe with
> corpses
> And from these graves arises
> an incredible hate
> Hate . . . everywhere!
> We are being consumed by hatred
> . . . without hope.
> We will all die . . . without hope . . .

This bloody turmoil, sown into Europe's heart, reaped a harvest of hate. A new hatred is arising from that same heart, one which is turning on Europeans themselves, leaving them to respond in a manner that reaches back into the hearts of the barbarian . . . Today, Europe is pushing people out, caught in a vice-grip of fear. The rhetoric of civilization, gleaned over an epochal moulding, felled in a few strokes.

Slavoj Žižek warns: 'A new dark age is looming, with ethnic and religious passions exploding, and enlightenment values receding.'[57] The prime minister of Hungary, Viktor Orbán, recently declared the end of 'liberal democracy' and vowed to build a new 'Christian democracy': 'The era of liberal democracy has come to an end. It is unsuitable to protect human dignity, inadmissible to give freedom, cannot guarantee physical security, and can no longer maintain Christian culture.'[58]

In 2019, at a Fourth of July celebration in Budapest, Orbán proclaimed that, with the presidency of Donald Trump, there was an 'overlap of values' between Hungary and the US: 'Neither of us is willing to accept the hypocrisy of modern politics, which neglects the fact that Christianity is the most persecuted religion globally.'[59]

Civilizational constructs are recast in medieval barbarism. It is fascinating to see these ideas get rapidly diluted as soon as the fragile constructs of culture are threatened. They seem based, not on extending an equal generosity, but in the essential idea of racial and cultural superiority.

The political consequences of treating refugees as the invasive other are immediate. Encampment, detention, forced repatriation, razor wire, search-

lights, guard patrols, and dogs all quickly follow.
[. . .] The United States had prided itself on
responding generously to surges in refugees and
forced migrants. During the Syrian civil war,
which has displaced nearly 10 million people, this
tradition lost its power to inspire public support
and guide policy. Since 2012, the United States has
taken in no more than fifteen thousand Syrian
refugees, and the newly elected president wants to
bar the door to any refugees from countries that
have a majority of Muslim citizens.[60]

A single image can suddenly overpower you with the force
of its violence, its tragedy. The iconic image of the three-
year-old boy washed ashore, his body inert, lying on the
vast expanse of the beach. Boats, ships, containers
crammed with people in inhuman conditions, casting their
cries, pleas, risking their lives, dying in the hundreds . . .
Two men in Italy caught in a legal battle because they
helped rescue migrants . . . the cruelty, the perversity of
'human' as opposed to 'humane' laws.

Île-de-France, or the Paris Region is the most
populous region of France covering only 2 per cent of the
country while at the same time accounting for nearly a
third of its GDP. Yet,

'What we've seen since 2010 in particular is a further concentration of wealth in the wealthy areas, while poverty has become more entrenched in the poorest areas' [. . .] The poorest areas are seeing 'a concentration of underqualified workers, often immigrants, with higher rates of unemployment or of precarious employment, and a growing number of single-parent households that have contributed to stigmatisation and deteriorating economic conditions.'[61]

John Berger and Jean Mohr's *A Seventh Man* (1975) examines the idea of 'emigration as capital export' and underscores the contribution of migrants to economies.

It has been estimated that the upbringing, the price of survival till the age of twenty of a migrant, has cost the national economy of his own country about 2000 pounds. With each migrant who arrives, an underdeveloped economy is subsidizing a developed one to that amount. Yet the saving for the industrialized country is even greater. Given the higher standard of living, the cost of 'producing' an eighteen-year-old worker at home is between 8,000 and 16,000 pounds.

> The use of labour, already produced else-
> where, means an annual saving for the metro-
> politan countries of 8,000 million pounds.
>
> To those who have machines, men are given.[62]

As aristocrats had armies of the poor to service them, carrying out degrading menial chores, so too do the wealthy nations have thousands of little men and women doing the jobs they no longer want to do.

The wants and desires of the West, its perceived insecurities, allow it to engage in war games, like wanton children kicking around battleships and submarines on their play boards. Unthought-out wars and alliances, the whole irresponsible adventurism of international diplomacy and policy, has created a Frankensteinian monster. Cosseted by decades of privilege, stability and power, utterly divorced from ground realities, so distanced from the lack that the Other suffers, the West yet presumes to speak for the Other. Parachuting into distant nations, vastly different cultures. From Afghanistan, through Iraq, Syria, Libya and beyond, into the messy regional power plays of Iran and Saudi Arabia, its self-indulgent lunacy has left in its wake not only millions dead but also many more millions devastated—homeless, helpless, battling distress and abject poverty. People want out, they want better lives. They want to live, and the only places worth living in now are Europe and the United States—the West. Why? Because of the relentless mischief, instability and violence these very powers have provoked across the world. Who then can deny the refugees, the migrants, their place in those worlds of safety, security and wealth?

8

HAJI: A BEAUTIFUL MAN

> And whatever I do
> will become forever what I've done.[63]

What is a man? Is he but a sum of his wanderings? An eventual embodiment of where he was forced to go or decided to take himself? At his journey's end, he leaves nothing but fragments of memories strung together by the threads of time.

I remember his face, his fine features, his eyes, his aura of one who is blessed at having achieved communion with the essence of the spirit, the light of his divine guide.

Haji. A beautiful man. If Maqsood was the man who fought against the world to achieve what was rightfully his, Haji negotiated the world on its own terms and came to an extraordinary accommodation within it.

Haji Aneesud Din. A man of the world, he told me of his dream. The realization of that dream cast a glow across his face, a peace settled across his features.

Haji and Maqsood. It is difficult to speak of one without mentioning the other.

'What can I tell you of my life? I have wiped the excrement of my employers' children, I have swabbed floors, but I had a dream and it was the constant hope of achieving that dream that kept me going.'

This revelation came as a shock to me. I was introduced to Haji by the principal of the local school who mentioned him as one of the most influential people in the colony. 'You must meet Haji-ji,' he said, 'if you want to know anything about Buland Masjid. He knows it best. He has done so much for the colony. In fact, he is on our board of trustees. I will see if he can drop in now, he lives next door.' A call was made and shortly after he arrived. Tall and well-built, with a grey beard, wearing a skullcap, a white kurta-pyjama and a shawl. He had a calm, gentle disposition and spoke with a strange, lilting sweetness.

Then followed a general discussion about the school and the colony. One of his first remarks, which remained with me, was about his joy and pride in the greening of the school. This was one of the few places in Buland Masjid where the periphery wall was surrounded by a cluster of young trees. With a twinkle in his eye, he told the principal, 'We have finally managed to get the MCD

(Municipal Corporation of Delhi) to water our plants and trees, which are doing very well now.' The principal turned to me and said, 'Haji-ji is the only one who knows how to get these things done.' It was wonderful to see the enthusiasm and pleasure that Haji felt in creating that small patch of green.

He said I should drop in and have a chat whenever I wanted. That was when he began to narrate the story of his life. From the balcony adjoining his sitting room, one could see the tall tenements of the colony, the minarets of the masjid prominent among them. He spoke of the colony's genesis and growth. A couple of visits later, he began with the story of his journey, his arrival at this destination.

'I belong to Amethi. My father was a well-to-do man, a prominent man in the village. We were wealthy. I remember, we had servants, the table was laden with food, we ate well, we lived well. My father was the Pradhan, he owned a fair bit of land which he would give out on "theka".

'The sudden death of my father changed everything overnight. From being the privileged children of the village, ensconced in security and comfort, we were faced with an uncertain and perilous future. My mother, a simple housewife, had to turn to others for guidance and help. Slowly she began to be fleeced by certain relatives and servants. We were all too young to understand anything, leave aside be of any help to her. Within no time, our fortunes began to deteriorate rapidly. We had a few kind relatives who stepped in to help out, but by then it was too late. Papers had been forged, lands and properties taken away, we had lost almost everything. It was at this breaking point that we began to think the unthinkable. For a long time, she refused. "No, never, it is just not possible, no child of mine will be sent off to work." It was terrible to watch her pain, her helplessness . . . I can never forget those nights. The sound of her muffled sobs, her crying, is imprinted in my brain.

'Obviously, I had been pulled out of school by then, but this trauma, this devastating upheaval taught me everything I needed to know about life and survival. In the face of this tremendous betrayal, this complete suspension of love and loyalty, the mendacity and dishonesty, I made a vow to myself: I will endure. Sheer hard work and absolute honesty will be the edifice on which I will build my life. I was only 10 when I took that pledge. The second but no less important lesson I'd learnt through these experiences was: money is not just an abstraction—

it is an inescapable fact. You have to make friends with the idea of money. It was a way of obtaining truth, honesty and justice. I was going to try and pull us out of poverty. I had already laid my dream out. I tell you this in all earnestness: I saw myself as a reasonably wealthy man, with a group of men around me, giving back to society, to the poor, the needy.'

He looked at me and smiled, 'I know you might be thinking I am narrating all this in hindsight, but I cannot emphasize how much this consumed my mind in those days of suffering.' There was a slight quiver in his voice.

'Anyway,' he continued, brushing off the moment of pain, 'the day eventually came when my mother could no longer put off the inevitable.' The 10-year-old was sent away to seek work in the big city.

'I well remember the day I left. The entire village came to see me off. Many had tears in their eyes, that a child who had grown up in my circumstances should have to see this day. My mother was inconsolable, but strangely, I was stoic, ready for what lay ahead.'

The 'big city' that Haji was taken to was not Delhi but Mumbai. 'My relative, who was taking me there, had some contacts who had promised to help.' This was his first foray out of his village in Amethi. The 10-year-old boy left the small rural outback to arrive at one of India's largest cities, Mumbai, the bustling, screaming megapolis of hope.

'And,' he recalls, 'Everything was black. There was no light to be seen, no street lights, car headlights, all black, all the buildings were just blocks of blackness.' The knot of fear that he carried within him was magnified several times over by these disturbing, alien conditions.

Young Haji had arrived in Bombay bang in the midst of the war between India and Pakistan. An account of the days of the blackout in Bombay by Michael Patrao:

> [A] series of red balls of fire had floated in the air moments after a blackout, and this was something the people had never before witnessed. Many thought it was the enemy bombing the city. [. . .] A few years later, I came to know that these orbs of fire were part of an anti-aircraft warfare to scare the enemy away during air raids. They were directed at a hostile aircraft to destroy them or chase them away. They posed a collision risk, making the attacker's approach more difficult.[64]

But the young Haji was clueless about it all. 'I don't know what had happened, I don't remember the year or even the circumstances. All I remember was that I was taken to a house and kept locked in for a week. The windows were pasted over with brown paper, the curtains were tightly drawn and we were not allowed to switch on any lights. The city was shrouded in darkness, no lights anywhere. Though I was not mistreated in any way, I was seized with a deep sense of fear. Here I was, so far away from my mother and family, with no means of communicating with anyone I knew, no one but the relative who had brought me here. During the day, he would go out, leaving me alone in the room. I would worry and fret till his return. Till this day, whenever I hear a siren, a shiver goes down my spine.'

'All I could do was to keep repeating to myself, like a mantra, "Keep strong, try hard to remember your resolve." I slowly adjusted to being alone, and looked to my relative for comfort and security. After a week in that room, I was taken to a place near Bhendi Bazaar. That is where I was left. I was handed over to a family, I remember, they were Memons. Now I was on my own with strangers.

'After discussing the terms of my service, my relative left. A salary of 15 rupees per month had been fixed. I would have to sweep and swab the floors, wash the clothes, take the elder child to school, look after the two younger children, their toilet, bathe them, dress them. I was a now a menial servant.'

Once again, the wry smile. 'It's all part of destiny.'

He remained in Mumbai for the next three years. 'As a city, I liked Bombay, I loved the buildings, there was a grandeur to it, there was life in that city.' In all those years he never went home, just kept sending his meagre earnings, his entire salary. 'Somehow, I would scrape together another five rupees for myself, and make ends meet.

'After three years of that, I was moved to Delhi. One day, someone came from my village and took me away. I just remember the sense of joy at moving closer to home and to finally be able to see my mother.'

It was here that he was to make his life.

He was brought to a place called Sarai Khalil, where he was employed in a 'hotel'. 'Now I was a dhaba boy and got 20 rupees a month. That's when I began to enforce my pledge to myself. I slogged as hard as I could, always retaining my integrity. My employer Bhai Yaqub, was a good, kind man. He saw my hard work. And for that he rewarded me, began to give me some extra money on the side. I had, as I said, nothing as such to recommend me, no real skills, but what I did have was my honesty. This he saw and understood. Within a year or two, he decided he could leave me in charge of his hotel and go to Faizabad where he wanted to expand his business. I kept the dhaba for him, sent the money to him. Once or twice a year, he would come to Delhi. We developed very good relations. When the time came, he helped me a great deal with my sister's marriage.

'After a while, I got thinking: if I can do this for someone else, why not take a place on rent and start my own business?

'I can tell you now that it was easier said than done. I managed to put together enough money to set up my own establishment. There were a series of travails. I was the victim of a local gang of goondas who got me evicted from my dhaba. I was helpless, they were very powerful people. I fled, with just the clothes on my back, and came to Jama Masjid.

'My old employer once again came to my rescue. By this time, I had discovered one thing about myself. While I had learnt no skills, what God had given me was a gift for cooking. Whatever I cooked would always be greatly appreciated. My employer understood my desire to establish my independence. He said to me, "You make great kheer, it is very famous among my clients. You just make kheer for me in the morning, and then you are free to do whatever you want." He suggested I set up a stall on the footpath near Dariba and sell some rice pulao. I would wake up at five in the morning to cook a potato tahri, 5 kilos of rice and 5 kilos of potatoes. All the rickshaw-walas and thela-walas used to come to me, and I would end up making 25–30 rupees. Then I would go and make the kheer. My employer would give me 40 rupees. In the evening, after five, I set up a rehri selling eggs. I remember, the police used to harass me, I would have to give them 5–10 rupees. Yet I would still earn 25–30 rupees. My daily earnings were about 100 rupees. In those days, that was a lot of money, people gave you respect if you were earning that kind of money. This was in 1984.

'In 1987, I came to Buland Masjid. I had saved 17,000 rupees. I invested it in land here. And it is from here that I began to realize my dream of being a successful man.

'My time in Delhi taught me something of great value. I had learnt and seen the nitty gritty, the economics of real estate, of land. I had seen, observed, how people operated, the politics of plot cutting, of carving out colonies, how land was used as a weapon, a tool. There was no logic to it—but there was acumen, there was cunning. My talent for cooking had brought me to this point. From this point on, I was going to use my knowledge to help me realize my dream. I knew that there were ways of doing this in an honest and straightforward manner.

'I am not boasting when I say this, it is a simple fact. But I found that there was something in me that earned the trust of people. People would come to me, ask me to intercede in their disputes, to arbitrate settlements, they would look to me for guidance, for advice.'

Haji's demeanour, his general mien was so kindly, so good-natured, his voice and manner calm, composed, it is easy to understand how he inspired such trust. There was something else: a certain pragmatism, a keen, sharp intelligence that knew how to rewrite the laid-down rules and edicts yet stay within the codes of a basic, native honesty. This is the book of life, and he draws his rules from it.

Talking to him, I get an insight into what marks this man out as different. His young daughter enters, bearing steaming cups of tea and biscuits. After she leaves, I ask if it is possible to help identify families who would be willing to let their daughters and wives be photographed. Without a pause, he tells me, 'Please, my family is there, I have no problems at all. Of course, I will tell you the names of other families, but you can start with mine.' Again, the wry smile, 'You see, within this colony are many kinds of people. By and large, no one imposes the purdah system. I have brought my girls up as equals with their brothers. But yes, within our community there is a great deal of discrimination, I don't subscribe to any of that kind of thing. In fact,' he grins, 'I have great quarrels with the Mullah-ji of one of the mosques here. They are a more conservative order, and he is relatively new to this colony. Even though none of us do so here, he has begun the practice of sacrificing camels on the auspicious occasion of Eid. He has no understanding at all. In this colony, where houses are crowded against each other, with open drains, you cannot have runnels of blood flowing down the narrow lanes. If we ourselves are disturbed by the sight of it, can you begin to imagine the plight of our Hindu brothers who live down that street? There are only a few of them there, but that is not the question. I have finally managed to convince him to stop the practice.'

He tells it lightly, glosses over it, but it is easy to understand the courage it must have taken to speak out, to defend the sensibilities of another community, of whom, in any case, there were very few in Buland Masjid, and to eventually prevail. This was a man who was not afraid to put himself forward and speak out for the other. I recall the SHO of Seelampur speaking of him, with a quiet respect, 'Haji-ji bahut nek insaan hain.' Haji-ji is a very good human being. 'Whenever we have a problem in the neighbourhood, I seek him out, knowing that he will always speak the truth and be fair.'

Haji applied his practical wisdom of the world to realize his dream. 'I built up a network that would inform me whenever they heard of anyone looking to sell land. I would trek to villages in what is Noida today, obtain lands from farmers, cut them into plots, organize them and then sell them. In Ghaziabad, here, in East Delhi, this is what I spent my time doing. The real-estate business was very profitable and soon I was doing well. I started looking further and doing the same thing in Amethi.

'I then decided to look towards the development of Buland Masjid. At that time, there was only Alamma Maqsood who had been tirelessly working for the colony and its people. I also began to get close to the politicians who would frequent this area, especially to Lovely-ji. I began to help in their campaigns. Working with the volunteers, preparing for the elections, going door to door, talking to people, I was with those who worked for Rahul-ji, Priyanka-ji and Sonia-ji. I had leverage in Amethi since it was my home turf and the people knew and loved me.' Amethi was the traditional stronghold of the Congress Party and the Nehru–Gandhi family, with Sonia Gandhi, Rajiv Gandhi and Rahul Gandhi successfully standing for elections there.

'I did not start out with the idea of committing my allegiance to a particular party. It's just that, while working for the colony, one had to push hard to get things done, and that could only be done through political representatives. No one was willing to enter this colony. I remember how hard we all had to work for our basic rights. This poverty, this filth, it was not right. It is criminal to treat men like animals. Alamma's fight for legalization of this colony is legendary. We also began to push for water, electricity, sewage and the school. Slowly, one by one, we managed to achieve our goals. But it was only pushed through by those who actually thought fit to venture in here, and to give him credit, that is what Lovely-ji did. And that is how I got close to him. Amethi was my home, he asked me to pitch in.'

Life had come full circle for Haji. The 10-year-old who had left to become a domestic worker in a household in Mumbai had now returned home, part of a political network instrumental in helping a man, and a political party, win the national elections. His eyes twinkle, he recalls, 'Mujhe raat ko phone aya Lovely-ji ka: Bhai bahut nazuk sthithi hai Amethi mein, tum jaldi jao aur kuch karo.' I got a call at night from Lovely-ji: It is a very delicate situation in Amethi. Please go there at once and do something.' I rushed there, mobilized all our forces, and by the grace of God, all went well, we were able to reach people, get our messages across and the result was there to see. We won that election.'

Haji looks mildly amused as he narrates his arduous trek to success, and, even though he does not underline it, to a certain power. He speaks fleetingly of another business he set up—a manufacturing unit that produced the much-in-demand jeans. He was, within his community, a wealthy, powerful man, now surrounded by a band of men who owed their allegiance to him. The dream that he saw as a little 10-year-old who had lost the world as he had known it; the world of love, security and comfort, that dream had now been realized.

'Main-ne hamesha ek sapna dekha ke mein jaa raha hoon, bas aise hi, aur mere saath char paanch log hain, aur main logon ki seva kar raha hoon. Bas yeh mera sapna tha aur yeh sapna sachai mein badal gaya.' I always had a dream that I was walking, with a retinue of four, five people, serving the public. That was my only dream and it has become a reality.

'But,' he adds, 'all of this does not mean so much as what I was able to do for my mother. I was able to finally wipe away her tears, those years of untold suffering, to return to her the respect she and her family were once held in within the village, among the people.

'For me, the most meaningful act of my life is the fact that I was able to fulfil my mother's greatest desire and take her on the Haj.'

The years of immense pain and struggle had not marked the man with any trace of bitterness. He is childlike in his belief in the innate goodness of mankind. 'By the grace of God, I have everything, and now we finally have our own graveyard here. I am at peace. People tell me I could easily shift to a better, more affluent colony, but I will never leave Buland Masjid. This is where I can hear the call of the azan, this is where I will be buried for my final rest.'

26 January 2016. There is a melee outside Haji's house. Huge crowds have gathered in the freezing morning cold. Haji's men are trying to impose order and get them to line up. Oblivious to the commotion, Haji stands in the midst of it all, smiling and gently handing out blankets and shawls to the men, women and children who have gathered there. He has reluctantly agreed to be photographed. 'I do not like to speak of this or publicize it in

any way. These are very poor people, they are needy and I abhor the idea of making a capital out of them.' This has been a tradition, a ritual he has followed ever since he was able to.

Haji, a beautiful man.

———————

2018. A slight illness and Haji breathes his last. His son tells me, 'The end was very peaceful. He was a man at peace with himself.' What about the ambitious project he was working on in Amethi? 'Yes, he completed that before he left. He set up a 250-bed hostel for the people.'

Haji in his final resting place. The graveyard faces his three-storied house where his family continue to live. Next to the graveyard is the school which he helped set up. His sons, well settled, manage the ever-expanding businesses and charities Haji had founded.

The people of the colony, ever moving, rushing, living out their lives of fragile fortunes, are now secure in the knowledge that a few good men have ensured that they will always have Buland Masjid to come home to. That is, at least in part, Haji's true legacy.

9

THE FINAL CHAPTER

Twelve million people in an unexpected mass migration fled their homes. Elsewhere in India, transfers of population took place on a smaller and less chaotic scale, but in all, an estimated 13 million people were uprooted from their homes. The Partition-related migrations represent the biggest refugee movement of the twentieth century. Many of the refugees left everything behind them in the chaotic two-way flight.[65]

The cyclical wanderings of this bloodied, ravaged sub-continent, where people are nothing but brittle pawns in the hands of the inheritors of new countries. Inheritors shorn of wisdom, compassion, intellect stripped of all intelligence. Inheritors of barbaric cruelty, they perpetuate migrations of hell. From a bitter Partition, these men take and impose an unbroken thread of suffering on a people who, 76 years into freedom, remain powerless, as weak and weary as they were when they ended their frenzied trudge. Still condemned to migrations, in search of the grail of freedom from fear, from hunger.

New Delhi, the capital city, crammed with the physical and emotional detritus of this upheaval.

The caravan returns,
it couldn't find the destination of desire.
There was only hope, and that too has faded.[66]

It has been the innate nature of the political maleficence that has governed this country after its founding to plunge its finger into the festering wounds of the disfranchised, the weak, the poor. These mini-cities are their playing fields.

In *Who are the Guilty?* (1984), a report published on the causes and impact of the Delhi Riots, a veteran politician based in Delhi is quoted as saying that the city's resettlement colonies 'are the rakhel (concubines) of the Congress (I)'.[67]

The brutish violence contained within this articulation, the inherent sense of contempt for human beings is but typical of the political temper that lurks within the governing classes across parties. And this city bears witness to the history of that inhumanity.

The 1984 killings saw the brutal murders of more than 3,000 Sikhs. The Muslim pogrom in Gujrat in 2002 saw this city absorb a fresh influx of desperate migrants seeking safety within Muslim ghettos like Zakir Nagar in Delhi.

Every so often these cities implode, fuelled by the indolent foot prods of whichever party that masquerades as the 'voice of the people'.

———

In 2014, violent clashes break out between 'two communities'. Tirlokpuri, once the centre of the Sikh killings, is now the site of another flashpoint created by the usual tinderbox of religion and the malice it is used for. Drunk boys, a scuffle, a bathroom, a dustbin, a mata ki chowki and, suddenly, arson, violence, more than 35 injured, including 13 policemen.

Vishva Hindu Parishad (VHP) leader Surendra Jain [on] Tuesday issued a warning to residents of Old Delhi's Hauz Qazi, where a communal flare-up had ended in the vandalism of a temple last week: 'Hum Hauz Qazi ko, Ballimaram ko Ayodhya banasakte hain . . . Ab Hindu pitega nahi, ye unko samajh lena chahiye (We can turn Hauz Qazi, Ballimaran into Ayodhya . . . Hindus will not be beaten any longer, they should understand this).'

Addressing the crowd, Akhil Bhartiya Sant Samiti general secretary Jitendra Nand Saraswati said, '[A]re Hindus of Delhi impotent? Delhi's Hindus are on the roads to tell that this is the last reaction. You did what you did, but don't force our hand. We will not migrate, and if they will force us, we will ensure they migrate from this country.'[68]

There it is again, the threat of more forced migrations.

———

17 December 2019, Buland Masjid. The freezing cold bites its way through the asphalt, into your feet, crawling up your legs as you walk through the narrow streets. It is one of the coldest days in Delhi in 50 years. There is a strange sense of vastness as you make your way through the drifting mist, the dim lights casting a grimy yellow tint to the sodden swirls of fog, laden with the blackness of tiny carbon particles that sear the lining of your eyes and your nasal passageways before settling in your lungs. Then it hits you— the streets are almost empty. Shutters are down. I ask Pir Baksh what is wrong. 'Yeh joh Seelampur mein ho raha hai.' The rioting that is going on in Seelampur. A stone's throw from this colony lies Seelampur where at that moment a pitched battle is being fought among the

residents and police. Stone pelting, arson and police firing on the protesting crowds. 'Sare log dar ke mare apne apne ghar mein bathein hain.' All the people are holed up in their homes in fear.

Across the road from Buland Masjid were the sub-divided complexities of the cities within cities of the chaotic rumpus of East Delhi. And the cities had erupted.

A controversial law, the Citizenship Amendment Act, unsettles deep historical fissures, spreading a tidal wave of fear across the country. The very question of belonging and security hanging by a thread.

The aftermath of Partition brought in its wake a frenetic fumbling that gave voice to a series of injunctions and laws, some of which may have erred in terms of clarity and justice.

The judgement asserted a narrative of Partition and its displacements in which Muslim refugees could only enter history by the fact of leaving. Citizenship was determined by Badruzzaman's departure, which was taken to legally constitute 'migration' and not by his 'ardent desire to return'. The judgement declared his claims of belonging through established familial ties as insufficient evidence of belonging to a nation.[69]

Yet a fig leaf can explain away the miscarriage of justice in the tumult of that particular time and circumstance.

Today, there is nothing, nothing at all that can explain away the loaded, twisted discriminatory laws. Within a new country, you are handed a mandate to start afresh and not scratch the scab of the past to undo self-perceived 'historical wrongs':

A child comes running
Looking scared, baffled and naive.
There's no one with him.
He has no acquaintance, friend or guardian.
He has no home, address or home town.[70]

From December 2019, the city, its people, politicians, the media—print, television and social—have been in the grip of a whipped-up, mythical battle, plunged deep into an orchestrated maelstrom with authoritarian echoes.

The tenor and nature of these new laws, as well as the old being used as weapons to subdue and muffle voices that seek to speak out against injustice and hate, awaken memories of the enactment of very similar laws almost a century ago by colonial powers aligned clearly against people of Indian origin. In South Africa, after the passing of the Asiatic Law Amendment Act (1907), 'All male Asians were required to register and be finger printed, and certificates (passes) were to be carried at all times. These certificates would have to be shown to police on demand.'[71]

The Indians held a mass protest meeting at Johannesburg in September 1906 and, under Gandhi's leadership, took a pledge to defy the ordinance if it became law in the teeth of their opposition and to suffer all the penalties resulting from their defiance. Thus was born satyagraha ('devotion to truth'), a new technique for redressing wrongs through inviting, rather than inflicting, suffering, for resisting adversaries without rancour and fighting them without violence [. . .][72]

And in British India, 'By February 1919, however, the British had insisted on pushing through—in the teeth of fierce Indian opposition—the Rowlatt Act, which empowered the authorities to imprison without trial those suspected of sedition.'[73]

Indians, a subject people, to be tamed and controlled by unhindered inhumanity. Gandhi's novel act of resistance, satyagraha, was in defiance of the 'enemy', the conqueror. It was a fight for freedom from centuries of slavery.

In 2019, in a corner of Delhi, we witness perhaps one of the most bizarre and naked demonstrations of injustice, a complete suspension of the very idea of justice. There is also a resonance of history. But the only difference is that the people are being forced into fear and distress by their very own. To protest against the controversial citizenship bill, a group of women take their cue from the father of the nation and sit at Shaheen Bagh in peaceful protest. They respect the law but the lawmakers do not. Using this peaceful protest as a trigger, the powers at the Centre unleash a cynically coordinated reign of terror that culminates in a vicious riot in the city.

24 February 2020. Smoke clouds push through the filthy haze of Delhi and up into the sky. Gunshots ring out, the roar of mobs. The earth is soaked with the blood of brothers. The police stand by watching, sometimes perpetrators, sometimes aiding and abetting the killers. By the end of February, over 50 people had been killed.

I think of the most famous migrant of this country, the returning native; who wanted a home, a country. These urban cities, these little choke-holes of mice and men, people of his home, his country. Where men prod and poke a severely injured man lying in his blood to sing the national anthem, a man who breathes his last the following day. Where men dump the butchered remains of their fellow men in the open sewers of shit flowing through the warren of mazes where they once lived their precariously built lives.

One man, and many others who walked with him, behind him. He built this fragile entity, with its savage discontents buffeting and pushing each other. But the fight was for transcendence, to vault over those savageries and start anew. It is difficult to ignore the loud shriek of history resounding through the chambers of justice.

In his last letter, one of India's great freedom fighters, Ram Prasad Bismil, writes before his hanging: 'Now my only request to countrymen is that if they had even an iota of sorrow at our death, then, with whatever means, they must establish Hindu–Muslim unity; that was our last wish and this only can be our memorial.'[74]

————————

In a tiny room, seven men sit. There is shock, there is horror. The bile of fear has once again risen from their guts, coursing its way upwards threatening to choke them. They are shaken, their eyes hold anxiety and anger, horror and helplessness. 'Hum ne aazadi yeh din dekhne ke liye nahin jeeti thi. Mussalman pe jo zulm ho raha hai . . . hum sirf chaahte hain ke koi yeh bill hamein samjhaye.' We did not win freedom to see such days. Muslims are being oppressed . . . all we want is that someone explain this bill to us.

Who gives a damn about that?

We are back to Maqsood, the eight-year-old boy whose life was a yearning to make peace with the epithet 'Tum Mussalman ho'.

EPILOGUE

Buland Masjid, where the poorest gather. A Muslim colony where Hindus live without fear. Throughout a long period of upheavals, it has remained free of hatred against the Other. 'We want to live without fear.'

Four years ago, the colony of Buland Masjid, along with the large field behind it, had been a riotous world of laughter. This was where Kashmiri migrants, too poor to withstand the bitter chill of winter at home, would make their annual stopover—a ritual that had been in place for more than 40 years—setting up brightly coloured tarpaulin tents, with warm carpeted interiors and walls draped with embroidered covers. Beautiful children ran wild, delighted by this annual adventure, a winterlude of joy. I had been engaged in documenting this seasonal migration for three years and, in the process, had developed a rapport with several of the Kashmiris, as they extended their warmth and hospitality, sharing cups of kahwa with me.

Clustered around the edge of the field are precarious hutments, the raw, crude beginnings of the urban dream. This is the refuge of Bihari and Bengali workers who divide their days between backbreaking labour and raucous respite in the winter sun.

But today, fear is inescapable. It is there in the eyes of my Kashmiri friends when they speak of Kashmir after the revocation of Article 370. 'Hamara bura hal hai, koi kaam nahin hai, log bhook se mar rahe hain. Pata nahin kya hoga hamara.' We are in a terrible state, there is no work, people are starving. We don't know what will happen to us. There is fear among the Bengalis and Biharis as well, 'We can't talk. Don't come here. They will take us away.'

<hr />

Across the white buildings beyond Buland Masjid, I see the Buddhist prayer flags of the Tibetan refugee colony; I see the crown of St James Church; the white dome of the Majnu ka Tila Gurudwara; and beyond, in the old city, the minarets of Jama Masjid. Across the river is Nigambodh Ghat, a place of reverence, of history, of sacredness, an ancient site where the gods themselves are said to have walked. A thousand migrations, hundreds of centuries, have gone into creating one of the most unique cities and cultures in the world. Today, new winds are blowing across the city, threatening to unravel a fabric woven through the ages.

Buland Masjid—where nothing is ever wasted, everything is used for a readying up, to start over. A never-ending cycle, as in the cycle of life, within the graveyard, where the earth has been turned over and over, as the remains of men mingle with those who came before them, and after. The raked mud, the deep red roses occasionally marking out fresh graves, heaped in a pile atop a mound of earth, petals everywhere. I am called, hailed out to, to come and look at the burial grounds from behind the tall gates. They want me to see this place of rest; there is pride in the graveyard. Rows of decorative streetlamps, painted a dull silver, line pathways through the grounds. They are switched on. In the falling light, in the last blush of the day, in this colony of endless melee, here is a place of tranquillity, of calm. Haji's words expressing his content, his peace, 'Yeh hamari iss duniya mein ek chota sa kona hai, yahan pe hum aazan ki aawaz sun sakte hain aur ab hamara qabarastan bhi ban gaya hai.' This is our little corner in this world. Here we can hear the call to prayer, and now we also have our graveyard. Maqsood and Haji both at rest in the paradise they created, their place of accommodation, their place of eternal rest.

Two men who sought light and love, and let their lives be guided by these. 'Idhar koi danga nahin hua hai, na hum hone deynge.' There has never been a riot here, nor will we allow one to occur. The void left by them, keenly felt within the colony.

Two men who understood the principle of justice, lived by it and built their extraordinary lives out of it.

'We don't know what we will do now. We miss their guidance in these troubled times.' As I sit with those who once walked with Haji and Maqsood, I feel the acuteness of the loss of the two men.

———

Today, a miasma of sadness seems to have slowly crept into Buland Masjid. A sense of neglect, of a griminess that pervades the colony. It is a dissipation of fortunes. This little city had been on an onward and upward march, visibly so as shops and homes replaced their filthy and precarious establishments with spanking new facades and interiors, building upwards but building stronger. There were weddings, celebrations, processions of men, women and children in bright, startling colours, gold and silver that twinkled and flashed, as they caught the bright lights, the women bedecked in dangling baubles—earrings, necklaces, bangles—happy, content, proud; tented pandals set up in every corner as enormous deghs on wood fires bubbled with kormas and cooks checked on the biryani, letting their smoky aromas out into the air. That festive air, the air of prosperity has vanished. The laughter of children, the young boys careering through the narrow lanes, the girls dressed to the nines in the latest fashions—they all seem to have left, leaving behind a pall of gloom, a strange desolation.

Hüzün, that is the word that suddenly comes to mind one day as I walk through the gallis. Once again, an association that seems incongruous and inappropriate for these surroundings, yet the word stays with me as I catch the eyes of old acquaintances. Hüzün, a quiet melancholy that has descended on this little city. In *Istanbul: Memories of a City* (2003), Orhan Pamuk's ode to his beloved city, the word is used with such great poetic impetus and force to describe the essential nature of the city.[75] I find a resonance, an echo, of the word when I look at Buland Masjid. A procession of men and little boys brushes past me softly, strangely quiet. I turn around. It is a janaza—a man, his face uncovered, bespectacled, not in a shroud but in a glass-topped casket, borne on a bier. Garlands of silver tinsel criss-cross and wrap themselves around his casket. I realize with a jolt that this is the first janaza that I have encountered during all my time here.

———

One of the most profitable occupations in Buland Masjid is what is known as 'lohe ka kaam'.

A welding establishment is fashioning bars of steel and turning them into what resembles a gate. Within a couple of days two gates have been completed and are slowly hauled up, then carried aloft to one of the many narrow entries into the colony. A few deft blows of a hammer, a welding gun and the heart sinks as it comprehends this new reality, Buland Masjid, the colony of migrants, the open city, has its first gates. It is now readying itself to face the new world.

When the war begins, it will be able to protect itself. The founding fathers have left. Their inheritors have been forced to submit to a new language. The language of fear.

———

These are the men; they have narrated their lives, bound by the essence of non-belonging, of outcastes walled off from the bounty of India's wealth. They have delved into the wellsprings of their fragile mortality to arrive here, to live this life. And they have celebrated this arrival.

Decades ago, in Old Delhi's Chandni Chowk, I spoke to a woman of over 90 years, who had survived the horrors of Partition. Her face had been sculpted into a beautiful visage by time that had been kind and benevolent. Her family loved the earth of this old country and could not bear to leave the air that carried the breath of their ancestors. She told me of the essence of Delhi. The 12 Khwajas had blessed this city. 'Dilli mein koi bhuka nahin jayega. Ab dekho, UP, Bihar, poore Hindustan se sab chale aate hain, koi bhuka nahin jaata.' No one will ever go hungry in Delhi. Just look, people come from UP, Bihar, all of India, and no one ever goes hungry.

Many years later, I find myself approached by a man in the chaos of Buland Masjid. He points to himself and says, 'Please take my photograph.' It is a face painful to behold. Every aspect of it is marked by deep suffering, unbearable sorrow. His eyes rheumy, his mouth turned down, not in bitterness but because he had forgotten how to smile.

His appearance would not be so wrenching but for the cap that he wore that somehow enhances his pain. A simple black knitted cap which bears, in large white letters, the word 'NICE'.

When I put my camera away and prepare to leave, after assuring him that I would hand him his photographs the next day, he suddenly calls out after me and, in a soft voice says, 'Dilli se mujhe apna haq nahin mila.' Delhi has not given me my due.

Those words resound with violence today. 'Dilli' is engaged in rewriting history. The blessing has been revoked. This city will now bless only the chosen people. No longer a refuge for the poor, the destitute.

On 25 March 2020, as the pandemic touches Indian shores, an edict is issued of a lockdown; people are given four hours to prepare for it. What ensues is a catastrophic exodus.

Tens of thousands of migrants are forced to leave the city and begin the long walk to their villages. Children die, mothers are forced to give birth on the highways' nowhere lands, they watch their infants die, infants sit by the side of dead mothers, men carry aged parents on their shoulders. It is a world that reflects indifference, cruelty, a total breakdown of humanity.

Why are they going back? 'Dilli mein ham sab bhukh se mar rahe hain. Ham ghar jayenge to kam se kam roti mil jayegi . . . ' We are dying of hunger in Delhi. If we go home, we will at least get a roti to eat.

Festering pits, piled with heaps of urban refuse spread their noxious fumes, while the residents lounge about in leisure, refusing to allow their surroundings to break their spirit. But how can any compassionate state create the circumstances that force its own people to live in such inhuman conditions?

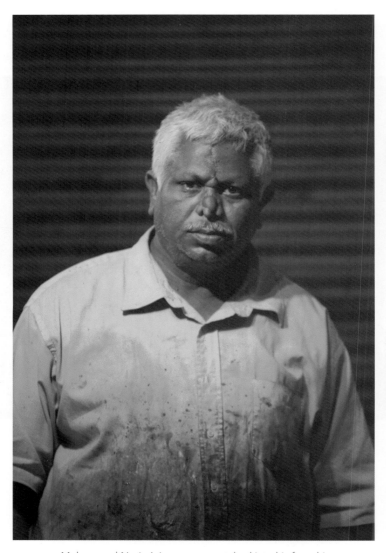

Mohammad Nazim's journeys are etched into his face, his memories marked by the darkness and light of the human condition.

Anees-ur-Rahman. His face . . . a painting by El Greco, suffering, piety and survival written into it.

Three generations of a family sit on a street lined with butchers' shops. The butchers' business is one of the most successful in Buland Masjid, along with the scrap dealers.

These pavements are etched with brutal stories of the lives of men and the marvel of reinvention that allows a man more than nine lives. Haré Baba seated at his takth.

A dreamy-eyed, whimsical mannequin, gazes out of the only
women's beauty parlour. Framed behind, Neha looks out
into the camera from the parlour owned by her mother.

Afsar Qureshi at his popular kebab shop.

Encounters with new ways of being, fascinate and create aspirations and desires to reach out to new worlds. Children at a local video parlour manoeuvre antique consoles, mesmerized by the adventures of exotic super heroes and villains.

A second generation of young women are not so bound
by the conservative way of life. They now take up work
outside the home. There is a sense of confidence,
contentment and joy within their expanding boundaries.

'Food, glorious food!' It is hunger that draws people here, and they have created a world where food is prevalent everywhere.

This is the world, the legacy of the two remarkable men,
'Allama' Maqsood (ABOVE) & Haji Anees-ud-Din (FACING PAGE),
and the many others, who strove to create and succeeded in
laying claim to a 'portion of the earth'.

They begin young, developing the insouciance, the style, that they display later as young men.

NOTES

1   John William Burgon, 'Petra' (1845) in *Poems* (*1840–1878*) (London: Macmillan and Co., 1885), p. 26.

2   Charles Olson, 'The Kingfishers' in *The Collected Poems of Charles Olson* (University of California Press, 1987), p. 87. Available online: https://rb.gy/rerko (last accessed: 17 July 2023).

3   Charles Darwin, 'Chapter 4: Comparison of the Mental Powers of Man and the Lower Animals—Continued' in *The Descent of Man, and Selection in Relation to Sex* (London: John Murray, 1871). Available online: http://rb.gy/5o620 (last accessed: 17 July 2023).

4   See Blake's illustrations of John Milton's *Paradise Lost* on *The William Blake Archive*: https://blakearchive.org/ (last accessed: 25 July 2023).

5   Genesis 4:9–12

6   'Tablet 1. The Coming of Enkidu' in *The Epic of Gilgamesh* (Andrew George trans. and intro.) (London: Penguin, 1999), p. 2.

7   Dhammapada, CHAP. 12: Attavaggo (The Self), v. 165. Translation found in Paul Carus, *Karma*: *A Story of Buddhist Ethics* (Chicago: Open Court, 1894), p. 40.

8   Jacob Bronowski, *The Ascent of Man* (London: BBC Books, 2011), p. 52.

9   Alice George, 'The Sad, Sad Story of Laika, the Space Dog, and Her One-Way Trip Into Orbit', *Smithsonian Magazine*, 11 April 2018. Available online: http://rb.gy/jl2u4 (last accessed: 17 July 2023).

10   Charles Baudelaire, 'The Voyage' in *Baudelaire: His Prose and Poetry* (Frank Pearce Sturm trans., Thomas Robert Smith ed.) (New York: Boni and Liveright, 1919), p. 97. Available online: http://rb.gy/xwy4k (last accessed: 17 July 2023).

11   V. S. Naipaul, *A House for Mr Biswas* (London: Pan Macmillan, 2016), p. 8.

12   Bruce Chatwin, *The Songlines* (London: Vintage, 1998), pp. 19, 271.

13   Charles Dickens, 'Chapter 6: New York' in *American Notes for General Circulation* (London: Chapman & Hall, 1913[1842]). Available online: http://rb.gy/irmq2 (last accessed: 18 July 2023).

14   See Stephen Johnson (1999), 'Past the Documents, to the Dance: The Witness to Juba in 1848' in Domenico Pietropaolo (ed.), *The Performance Text* (Ottawa: Legas, 1999), pp. 78–96. Available online: http://rb.gy/be7dk (last accessed: 18 July 2023).

15 Kevin Baker, 'The First Slum in America', review of *Five Points* by Tyler Anbinder, *The New York Times*, 30 September 2001. Available online: http://rb.gy/pc7no (last accessed: 18 July 2023).

16 Dickens, 'Chapter 6: New York' in *American Notes*.

17 Letter reprinted in Trevor Blount, 'Dickens's Slum Satire in Bleak House', *The Modern Language Review* 60(3) (1965): 340–51; here, pp. 342–43. Letter also available online on the *Victorian Web*: http://rb.gy/8vnkj (last accessed: 18 July 2023).

18 George Bernard Shaw, Letter to Siegfried Trebitsch (18 November 1902) in *Collected Letters: 1898–1910* (Dan H. Laurence ed.) (New York: Viking, 1985), p. 288.

19 Frederick Engels, 'The Great Towns' in *The Condition of the Working Class in England* (Florence Kelley Wischnewetzky trans.) (London: Allen & Unwin, 1892). Available online: http://rb.gy/yzi9d (last accessed: 18 July 2023).

20 Rumi, quoted in the translator's epigraph to Attar, *The Conference of Birds* (Sholeh Wolpé trans.) (New York: W. W. Norton, 2017).

21 Terry, played by Marlon Brando, in *On the Waterfront* (1954), directed by Elia Kazan and written by Budd Schulberg.

22 Charles Baudelaire, 'Parisian Dream' in *Flowers of Evil* (Edna St. Vincent Millay trans.) (New York: Harper and Brother, 1936). Available online: http://rb.gy/eysb8 (last accessed: 18 July 2023).

23 Sean Bonney, 'Rêve parisien' in *Baudelaire in English* (London: Veer Books, 2018).

24 Interview with Robert Frost, *Public Ledger* (Philadelphia), 4 April 2016.

25 Press Trust of India, 'Man arrested in 2006 murder case', *Moneycontrol*, 3 February 2012. Available online: http://rb.gy/mzk27 (last accessed: 20 July 2023).

26 Charles Dickens, 'Chapter 5: The Wine-shop' in *A Tale of Two Cities: A Story of the French Revolution* (London: Chapman & Hall, 1859). Available online: http://rb.gy /13085 (last accessed: 20 July 2023).

27 François Rabelais, *The Histories of Gargantua and Pantagruel* (J. M. Cohen trans.) (New York: Penguin Books, 1955), BOOK 1, CHAP. 17.

28 Dominique Laporte, *History of Shit* (Nadia Benabid and Rodolphe el-Khoury trans) (Cambridge, MA: MIT Press, 2002), p. 26.

29 Charles Baudelaire, quoted in Walter Benjamin, *Selected Writings: Volume 4, 1938–1940* (Howard Eiland and

Michael W. Jennings eds) (Cambridge, MA: Belknap Press of Harvard University, 2003), p. 48.

30   Mike Davis, 'Slum Ecology', *Orion Magazine* 25(2) (March/April 2006). Available online: http://rb.gy/n637c (last accessed: 20 July 2023).

31   Ambika Pandit, 'Mapping exercise holds key to fate of 1,797 colonies', *The Times of India*, 25 April 2018. Available online: http://rb.gy/6o25z (last accessed: 28 August 2023).

32   Delhi Development Authority, *Master Plan for Delhi 2021* (*Incorporating modifications up to 31 December, 2020*) (2007–2020). Available online: http://rb.gy/6xxt1 (last accessed: 20 July 2023).

33   'Delhi Population 2023', *World Population Review*. Available online: http://rb.gy/hd4kw (last accessed: 28 August 2023).

34   Calculated at 55 per cent of 97,790.90 hectares available for residential use, see 'Table 1.0: Availability of Urbanisable Land in NCT - Delhi for 2021' in Delhi Development Authority, *Master Plan for Delhi 2021*, p. 10.

35   *A People's Housing Policy: The Case Study of Delhi* (New Delhi: Hazards Centre, 2003), p. 25.

36   Chitvan Gill, 'Housing: The Future is a Ghetto', *Urban Futures Initiative*, 26 May 2005. Available online:

http://rb.gy/xm15e (last accessed: 28 August 2023). The article uses data from Bijit Ghosh, 'Delhi: The Expanding Metropolis I', 15 March 1971 (personal archive). A more recent commentary notes, 'By 1978, the Authority planned to have developed 30,000 acres for residential use, it only succeeded in developing 13,412 acres': Shabana Sheikh and Ben Mandelkern, 'The Delhi Development Authority: Accumulation without Development', Centre for Policy Research (2014), p. 3.

37 The *Master Plan 2021* projected a shortage of 2 million units, and a backlog of 400,000 units. Delhi Development Authority, *Master Plan for Delhi 2021*, p. 32.

38 Abhijit Banerjee, Rohini Pande and Michael Walton, 'Delhi's Slum Dwellers: Deprivation, Preferences and Political Engagement among the Urban Poor', International Growth Centre (2012), p. 1.

39 Pandit, 'Mapping exercise holds key to fate of 1,797 colonies'.

40 Statement of the Minister of State for the Ministry of Housing and Urban Affairs: 'The motion for consideration of the National Capital Territory of Delhi (Recognition of Property Rights of Residents in unauthorised Colonies) Bill, 2019 (motion adopted and bill passed)', Seventeenth Lok Sabha, 7 September 7 2022, p. 4. Available online: http://rb.gy/hfsds (last accessed: 28 August 2023).

41 Amarnath Tewary, 'If we don't migrate, we will starve to death here', *The Hindu*, 15 December 2019. Available online: http://rb.gy/z4b04 (last accessed: 20 July 2023).

42 Davis, 'Slum Ecology'.

43 Sigmund Freud, *Civilization and Its Discontents* (Joan Riviere trans.) (London, Hogarth Press: 1930), p. 56.

44 Davis, 'Slum Ecology'.

45 Mike Davis, *Planet of Slums* (London: Verso, 2006), p. 19.

46 Davis, 'Slum Ecology'.

47 Charles Dickens, 'On Duty with Inspector Field', *Household Words* 64 (1851).

48 Dorothea Lange, quoted in Milton Meltzer, *Dorothea Lange: A Photographer's Life* (Syracuse, NY: Syracuse University Press, 2000), p. 133.

49 Dorothea Lange, *Destitute pea pickers in California. Mother of seven children. Age thirty-two. Nipomo, California* (United States Nipomo San Luis Obispo County California, March 1936). Available online at the Library of Congress: www.loc.gov/item/2017762891/ (last accessed: 24 July 2023).

50 Interview with Florence Thompson by Bill Ganzel (c.1930s), quoted in Errol Morris, 'The Case of the Inappropriate Alarm Clock (Part 7)', *The New York Times*,

24 October 2009. Available online: http://rb.gy/lh4dk (last accessed: 24 July 2023).

51 Interview with Katherine McIntosh by Thelma Gutierrez and Wayne Drash, 'Girl from iconic Great Depression photo: "We were ashamed"', *CNN*, 3 December 2008. Available online: http://rb.gy/qnnmb (last accessed: 24 July 2023).

52 Theodore Dalrymple, 'Lost in the Ghetto' in *Life at the Bottom* (Chicago, IL: Ivan R. Dee, 2001), pp.155–56.

53 Percy B. Shelley, *Hellas: A Lyrical Drama* (London: Charles and James Ollier, 1822), p. 50.

54 See the official website of the German exhibition at the 2016 Venice Biennale of Architecture for more information: http://rb.gy/xdd1d (last accessed: 25 July 2023).

55 Stefan Dege, 'Making Heimat: Germany at Venice's Architecture Biennale', *DW*, 30 May 2016. Available online: http://rb.gy/2xenk (last accessed: 25 July 2023).

56 John Gray, 'Steven Pinker is wrong about violence and war', *The Guardian*, 13 March 2015. Available online: http://rb.gy/ey95v (last accessed: 25 July 2023).

57 Slavoj Žižek, 'Anger in Bosnia, but this time the people can read their leaders' ethnic lies', *The Guardian*, 10 February 2014. Available online: http://rb.gy/9oxit (last accessed: 25 July 2023).

58 Kovács András, 'Orbán Viktor negyedszerre is Magyarország miniszterelnöke' [Viktor Orbán is the Prime Minister of Hungary for the fourth time], *Origo*, 10 May 2018. Excerpts of the speech are available in English translation in 'Orban declares end of "liberal democracy" in Hungary, vows to fight for Christian values', *RT International*, 10 May 2018 (available online: http://rb.gy /dy4om; last accessed: 25 July 2023).

59 Shaun Walker, 'Orbán deploys Christianity with a twist to tighten grip in Hungary', *The Guardian*, 14 July 2019. Available online: http://rb.gy/ri3b9 (last accessed: 25 July 2023).

60 Michael Ignatieff, 'The Refugee as Invasive Other', *Social Research* 84(1) (Spring 2017): 223–31; here, p. 224.

61 Claire Mufson, 'Rich and poor increasingly segregated in Paris region', *France 24*, 3 June 2019. Available online: http://rb.gy/kyudu (last accessed: 25 July 2023).

62 John Berger and Jean Mohr, *A Seventh Man*: *Migrant Workers in Europe* (Harmondsworth: Penguin, 1975), pp. 68–69.

63 Wisława Szymborska, 'Life While-You-Wait' in *Map*: *Collected and Last Poems* (Clare Cavanagh and Stanisław Bara czak trans) (Boston, MA: Houghton Mifflin Harcourt, 2015), p. 229.

64 See Michael Patrao's 'Memories of 1971' (*Deccan Herald*, 15 March 2019) for an account of Bombay during the 13-day war. Available online: http://rb.gy/bqk88 (last accessed: 25 July 2023).

65 Darshan Singh Tatla, 'Rural roots of the Sikh Diaspora' in Ian Talbot and Shinder Thandi (eds), *People on the Move*: *Punjabi Colonial, and Post-Colonial Migration* (New Delhi: Oxford University Press, 2004), pp. 45–62; here, p. 61.

66 Akhtar-ul-Iman, 'Deprivation' in *Query of the Road* (Kathleen Grant Jaeger and Leslie Lavigne trans, Baidar Bakht ed.) (ed.) (New Delhi: Rupa, 1996), p. 36.

67 People's Union for Democratic Rights and People's Union for Civil Liberties, *Who are the Guilty? Report of a joint inquiry into the causes and impact of the riots in Delhi from 31 October to 10 November 1984* (New Delhi, 1984), p. 4. Available online: http://rb.gy/c6327 (last accessed: 25 July 2023).

68 Abhinav Rajput, 'On day 3 BJP MPs visit temple, VHP leader says: Can turn Hauz Qazi, Ballimaran into Ayodhya', *The Indian Express*, 10 July 2019. Available online: http://rb.gy/aa2hj (last accessed: 25 July 2023).

69 AIR (38), 1951 Allahabad 16, *Badruzzaman v. The State*, discussed in Vazira Fazila-Yacoobali Zamindar, 'Refugees,

Boundaries, Citizens' in *The Long Partition and the Making of Modern South Asia* (New Delhi: Viking, 2008), p. 108.

70 Akhtar-ul-Iman, 'Resolve' in *Query of the Road*, p. 566.

71 'Asiatic Law Amendment Act is passed in Transvaal parliament leading to increased Indian protest under MK Gandhi', *South African History Online*, 19 March 2009. Available online: http://rb.gy/fyrza (last accessed: 25 July 2023).

72 B. R. Nanda, 'Gandhi, Mahatma', *Encyclopedia Britannica*, 17 September 2023. Available online: http://rb.gy/tp535 (last accessed: 19 September 2023).

73 B. R. Nanda, 'Mahatma Gandhi', *Encyclopedia Britannica*. Available online: http://rb.gy/2ehyp (last accessed: 25 July 2023).

74 Read the letter reprinted in *National Herald*: http://rb.gy/4a59w (last accessed: 25 July 2023).

75 Orhan Pamuk, *Istanbul: Memories of a City* (Maureen Freely trans.) (Kent: Faber and Faber, 2005), p. 79.